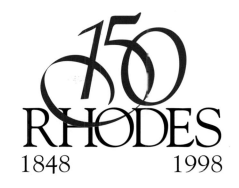

A Sesquicentennial Yearbook

BUCKMAN HALL

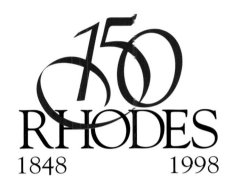

150

RHODES

1848   1998

A Sesquicentennial Yearbook

Bennett Wood

August House Publishers, Inc.

LITTLE ROCK

Published 1998 by August House, Inc.,
P.O. Box 3223, Little Rock, Arkansas, 72203,
501-372-5450.

Printed in Hong Kong

10 9 8 7 6 5 4 3 2 1

LIBRARY OF CONGRESS CATALOGING-IN-PUBLICATION DATA

Wood , Bennett , 1932 —
    Rhodes 150 : a sesquicentennial yearbook / Bennett Wood .
    p .   cm .
    Includes bibliographical references and index .
    ISBN 0-87483-538-0
    1 . Rhodes College — History . 2 . Rhodes College — Pictorial works .
    I . Title .
    LD4707 . W66 1998
    378 .768' 19 — dc21   98-27462

Book design by Alchemy Design and Harvill Ross Studios Ltd

AUGUST HOUSE, INC. • PUBLISHERS • LITTLE ROCK

Contents

"Dear Alma Mater, kind the fate that links our lives with Thee . . ."

Like a family album, this 150th anniversary pictorial history brings our collegiate ancestors to life, those who helped give shape and form to the institution we call Rhodes.

In their hands a vision persisted—from Clarksville Academy to Masonic University, Montgomery College, Stewart College, and Southwestern Presbyterian University; then on to Memphis, to Southwestern, and to Rhodes—a monument to genuineness and excellence.

Dr. Diehl's words upon the College's opening in Memphis in 1925 still resonate today to Rhodes' steadfast purpose:

She holds aloft the unpurchasables as objects of desire and bears an unfaltering testimony to the value of spiritual ideals. She seeks to prepare for generations yet unborn by handing down unsullied to this generation our rich heritage of the past. She labors to send out men and women with strong characters and disciplined minds which are to be put at the disposal of the world's need for the solution of its desperate problems, for the alleviation of its myriad ills, and for the bringing of that better day when wrong shall cease, and liberty and love and truth and right o'er all the earth are known as in their throne above.

As we celebrate our College's sesquicentennial anniversary, our hearts are filled with humility, gratitude, and pride. Humility, because we are the beneficiaries of those men and women of vision who have nurtured this institution since 1848. Gratitude, because the College has remained true to its mission and values since its inception. And pride, because at 150 years of age, the College has never been stronger.

Godspeed, Rhodes College.
. . . fare forward, voyagers.

James H. Daughdrill, Jr.

James H. Daughdrill, Jr.
President

"I am looking at a perpetuity"

The Rollow Avenue of Oaks, which leads from North Parkway to Diehl Court and Palmer Hall, is named in honor of John A. Rollow '26, who devoted his life to the College as Supervisor of Property and College Engineer from 1926 until 1968. It was he who brought the oak seedlings from the original campus in Clarksville and planted them on the new campus.

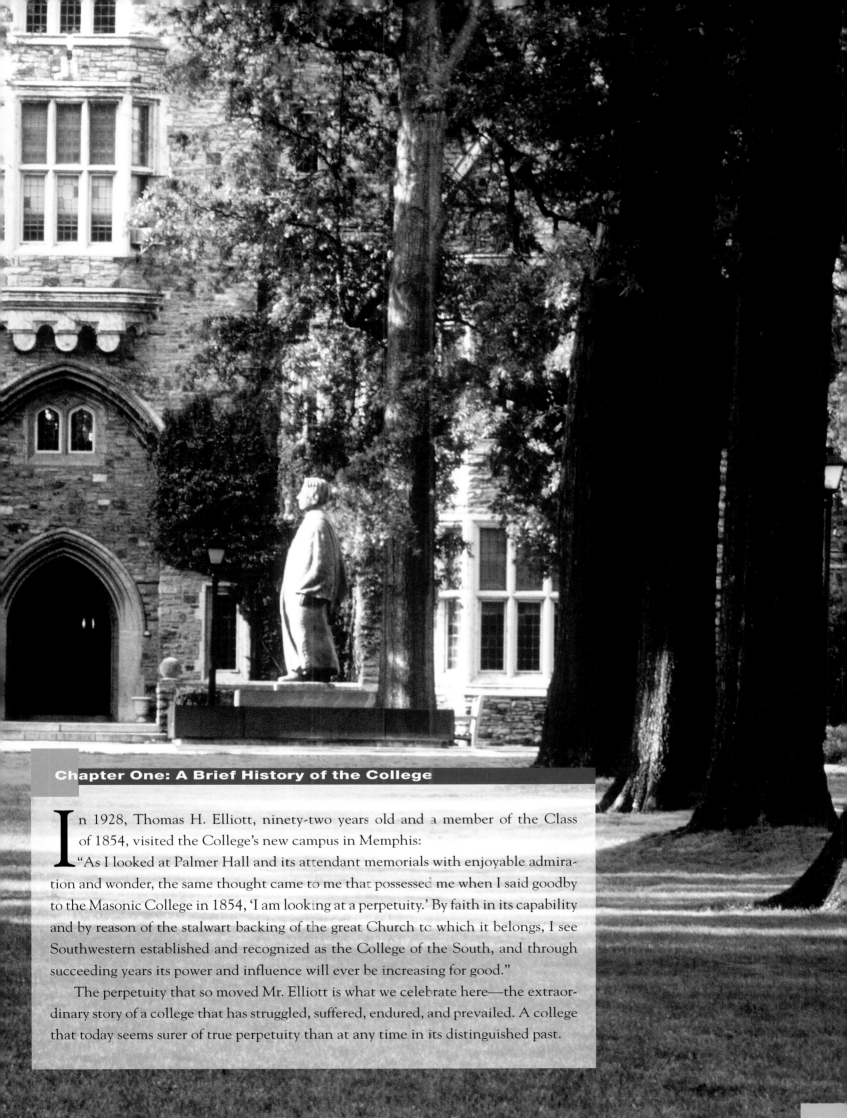

Chapter One: A Brief History of the College

In 1928, Thomas H. Elliott, ninety-two years old and a member of the Class of 1854, visited the College's new campus in Memphis:

"As I looked at Palmer Hall and its attendant memorials with enjoyable admiration and wonder, the same thought came to me that possessed me when I said goodby to the Masonic College in 1854, 'I am looking at a perpetuity.' By faith in its capability and by reason of the stalwart backing of the great Church to which it belongs, I see Southwestern established and recognized as the College of the South, and through succeeding years its power and influence will ever be increasing for good."

The perpetuity that so moved Mr. Elliott is what we celebrate here—the extraordinary story of a college that has struggled, suffered, endured, and prevailed. A college that today seems surer of true perpetuity than at any time in its distinguished past.

13

Masonic University of Tennessee

On December 5, 1848, the Board of Trustees of the Masonic University of Tennessee held its first meeting in Clarksville and resolved "to proceed at once with the organization of the institution, both in its preparatory and collegiate departments."

And proceed they did, with all due speed. A faculty of six was hired and in place by January 1, 1849, and classes began on that day.

The Board of Trustees was carrying out the wishes of the Grand Lodge of the Masonic Order of Tennessee, which had determined that it would be to the greater glory of their organization to establish and support a first-class college. Such a college would offer higher education to the young men of the state and provide an opportunity for the charitable impulses of the Masonic lodges across the state. It was a noble cause, conceived in generosity and largeness of spirit.

Clarksville was chosen as the site for the new Masonic institution due largely to the efforts of the Clarksville Masonic Lodge, which was eager to have the distinction of bringing a university to their town. Clarksville and the other lodges of Montgomery County actively campaigned for the selection and offered to provide the College with the building then housing the Clarksville Male Academy (most of the members of the Academy Board were Masons). This building was a "fine two-story brick house, capable of accommodating 100 students," on a five-acre tract near the northern edge of Clarksville, "in a beautiful grove of native forest trees, on a gently elevated but commanding position."

The Clarksville and Montgomery County Masons had also agreed to raise and contribute at least $15,000 toward the erection of a new college building. And on February 22, 1849, with a fine flourish of nineteenth-century American oratory, the leaders laid the cornerstone for this building. In the stone were deposited the Masonic proceedings authorizing the College, a copy of the Masonic monthly journal, an almanac and some coins of the current year, a scroll on which were inscribed the names of national, state and town government officials, and a list of

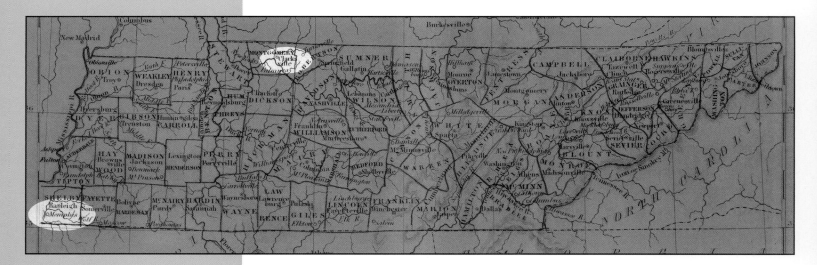

Just sixty miles northwest of Nashville along the Cumberland River, Clarksville achieved its initial prosperity from the iron-ore deposits in the nearby hills and the rich soil that yielded a particularly strong dark-fired tobacco with a seven percent nicotine content. In this 1835 map, note that Memphis is indicated as the smaller of the two towns in Shelby County and Raleigh as the larger.

1848

The "Year of Revolution" in Europe.

Louis Philippe deposed in Paris, uprisings in Vienna, Prague, Madrid, Rome.

Treaty of Guadeloupe Hidalgo ends the Mexican-American War, gives the United States Texas, New Mexico, California, Nevada, Utah, Arizona, parts of Colorado and Wyoming.

Discovery of gold in California leads to the '49 gold rush.

First U.S. women's rights convention meets in Seneca Falls, New York.

Wisconsin becomes a state.

Karl Marx and Friedrich Engels publish *The Communist Manifesto*.

John Stuart Mill publishes *Principles of Political Economy*.

Grand Lodge and local Masons. According to the Masonic chronicler, as the baptismal oil was poured on the cornerstone, "the canopy of cloud vanished and the sun shone forth in radiant splendor."

This propitious omen, alas, was not an accurate prediction of the future for the infant institution. For soon after the new building was completed in 1850, the state Grand Lodge withdrew its support from the College. Several other Tennessee local Masonic orders had decided to form colleges in their own towns rather than support the Clarksville one, so the Masonic Order of Tennessee found itself unable to carry out its commitment. The Masonic lodges of Montgomery County were now the sole financial backer.

Clarksville's site on the banks of the Cumberland River, plus its gently rolling terrain and abundance of good spring water, attracted settlers as early as 1780. Although early settlements were destroyed by Indian raids,

This unique turreted building at the edge of town would seem to be the recently completed home of the Masonic University.

A Rural Academy

In 1806 the Tennessee legislature established in each of the twenty-seven counties of the state a "Land Grant" academy. Equivalent to contemporary K-12 schools, these academies were supported by a combination of state funds, subscriptions, and fees, and were primarily for male students only.

In Clarksville, "Rural Academy" was chartered and located on the edge of town at Washington (later College) Street and Henry Street, on a tract purchased from H. Robb. One of the five trustees of the new academy was Willie Blount, who soon thereafter served three terms as Governor of Tennessee from 1809 to 1815.

The site of Rural Academy has remained dedicated to higher education from its founding to this day, even though the name and purpose of the institutions have varied with the time.

Rural Academy—1806-1811

Mount Pleasant Academy—1811-1825

Clarksville Academy—1825-1848

In 1848 the academy property was offered to the Grand Lodge of Tennessee Masons for use as a college.

in 1784 John Montgomery bravely laid out a town plan and the town was established by the North Carolina legislature on December 29, 1785. It was named for the Revolutionary War hero General George Rogers Clark. By 1796, when Tennessee achieved statehood, the surrounding county had a population of 1,941 and plans were underway for a courthouse, a prison, and stocks. When this drawing was made in the 1850s, the population was 2,600.

Montgomery Masonic College

When the College opened its session in 1851 in its splendid new castellated building, it did so under a new name. No longer the ambitiously titled Masonic University of Tennessee, it was now more modestly called Montgomery Masonic College.

The faculty set to work writing the rules and regulations of the new College and in 1853 published what would seem to be its first catalogue, detailing the courses of study offered, and spelling out the students' hours of study, their duties and responsibilities, and the punishments they could expect to receive for any infractions of rules or derelictions of duty. The catalogue also included the names of the faculty (there were seven) and all the students (46 in the College, 116 in the Preparatory School).

But soon after the catalogue of 1853-54 was published, the College found that its debts were mounting faster than the Masonic lodges were able to meet them. Stronger sponsorship had to be found.

The man on whom this responsibility fell was the President of the College, William M. Stewart, a native of Philadelphia who had come to Tennessee as a scientist/businessman and made a substantial fortune in the iron business. Involved with the College first as a supporter and contributor, he soon joined the faculty (without pay) as a Professor of Natural History and was asked to be President in 1853.

As a Presbyterian elder, President

The first catalogue for Stewart College in 1855 spelled out the rules of behavior for students . . . and the punishment for infractions.

CATALOGUE.   13

SECTION SECOND.
CLASSIFICATION OF DEMERITS AND PUNISHMENT.

1. Offences against good morals, order, and discipline are arranged in three classes.

2. The first and highest grade of offences are: profanity, fighting, carrying of dangerous weapons, gambling, drunkenness, riot, disturbance of public worship, deliberate falsehood, combination to resist discipline, etc. These and such like offences usually infer the expulsion of the offender.

3. The second grade are: disrespectful behavior to a teacher, throwing dangerous missiles, visiting improper places, continuing neglect of study after warning, wanton damage to the buildings or property of the College, going out of town without permission, being out of lodging at night, etc.

4. Offences of the third grade are: light behavior during worship, disorderly behavior in the street, scuffling or unnecessary noise in or near the College, attempts to create laughter during recitations or otherwise disturb them, prompting during recitations, etc.

5. The above is not intended for a complete catalogue of offences, but merely for an indication of the mode of classifying them. It may suffice to state in general terms, that whatsoever is contrary to good morals, good order, or the purposes for which shools were established, is forbidden by the laws of this institution.

6. The number of demerits attached to each offence is left to the discretion of the President.

7. The grades of punishment are Expulsion, Dismissal, and Probation.

ARTICLE SIXTH.

1. The prices of tuition are as follows:

Stewart was well aware of the great importance his church attached to education, so it was to that church he went in search of support for his ailing College. In 1855, his church responded by purchasing the buildings, grounds and other possessions of the College in the name of the Synod of Nashville. In honor of the man who had served the College so devotedly in its early years, the Board of Trustees changed its name to Stewart College.

Stewart College

Under its new sponsorship and its new name, the College hoped to achieve a measure of stability it had not previously enjoyed. With enough money on hand for day-to-day operations, the establishment of an endowment fund soon become a priority. President Stewart and his faculty had established a reputation for high academic standards, but Stewart's rather retiring nature made him uncomfortable with the aggressive work of raising endowment money. Consequently, in 1858 he resigned from the presidency and the Board selected as his replacement a Presbyterian minister and former chemistry professor from Knoxville, the Rev. R.B. McMullen, D.D.

President McMullen's fundraising activities were eminently successful. By 1860, gifts and pledges assured that the proposed endowment would be fully subscribed, and the College looked forward with optimism to a secure future.

And then came April 1861, Fort Sumter, and the Civil War.

In July of that year, President McMullen placed a notice in the Clarksville *Jeffersonian*, a local paper, that despite the departure of most of the student body for the army, exercises would resume in September for the younger students: "We earnestly hope that before September our invaders will have received such salutary lessons as will induce them to remove their polluting feet from our sacred soil, so that teachers and pupils may return to their literary and scientific pursuits. But if in this we are disappointed, we will wait till our brethren and fellow-students shall have taught the President and his Cabinet to march from Washington in a still more lively double-quick step than they employed in marching to it."

The earliest known representation of the college's first building, the Castle, was this engraving on the College's stationery in the 1850s.

William A. Forbes
Teacher and Warrior

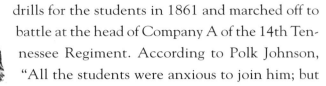

Col. Forbes, a Virginian by birth, was Professor of Pure and Mixed Mathematics at Stewart College from the founding of the College in 1848 to the onset of hostilities between the North and South. He also served as President of the College from 1851-53. Having had some military training in his native state, he organized and led military drills for the students in 1861 and marched off to battle at the head of Company A of the 14th Tennessee Regiment. According to Polk Johnson, "All the students were anxious to join him; but he would not allow the boys to go to war without the consent of their parents." Forbes was killed in August, 1862, at the second battle of Manassas, "while bravely leading the regiment in a charge against the enemy's batteries."

"It seems to me impossible to continue the exercises of the College..."

President McMullen struggled to keep the College going with its Preparatory School classes during the first year of this "desolating war." But with all the collegiate students gone, there was not enough income from tuition to maintain a staff, as is evidenced by this letter to the Board of Trustees in September 1862.

McMullen also described to the Board of Trustees what happened to the principal college building, the Castle, when it was commandeered by federal troops when they took control of Clarksville:

"The conduct of these last while occupying the College building was characterized by the grossest vandalism. Notwithstanding their solemn and oft repeated promises to respect and protect the property, they themselves, yes, the very officers who made these promises, four several times forced the doors of the cabinet rooms, broke open the cases of mineralogical and geological specimens and carried away many of the most valuable specimens, and choice portion of the books belonging to the Washington Irving Society, chairs, tables, curtains, etc., finally stripping even the College chapel of everything in it."

Estimating the damage done to the Castle at more than $10,000, McMullen expressed a hope that "this amount of damages may yet be obtained in some way through our Government." After the war, claims were filed against the federal government and the College was finally awarded damages in the amount of $25,000—in 1904.

To The Trustees of Stewart College, Gentlemen:

The present prospects of the Country are such, in view of our desolating war, that it seems to me impracticable to continue the exercises of the College without such an improvement in its financial resources as I cannot now anticipate. It has pleased God to afflict us sorely for the present for our good. But out of it all we shall come forth purer & brighter than before. For the present, however it seems to me hopeless for me to continue the exercises of the Institution with

Alfred Robb

Robb was an early volunteer in the Confederate army and was elected to be Lieutenant-Colonel of the 49th Tennessee Regiment. He was mortally injured in the Battle of Fort Donelson on February 15, 1862, as described in this account by Polk G. Johnson:

"No braver or better soldier or man ever died. He went into the battle upon a large white horse, and being himself a very large man (nearly seven feet tall), was a fine target for sharpshooters. He was shot through the breast by one of these, and when shot put his hand on his breast, and saying he was shot started to the rear. Several men followed him and he would have fallen from his horse in fifty yards but for their assistance. The men managed to get him to his quarters. During the night he was carried to the boats at Dover to be sent to Clarksville with the other wounded. Two boats were at the wharf, one fastened to the bank and the other on the side of this boat. He was placed on the first boat to be carried through to the second; in crossing from the one to other the boats separated—the men holding his legs let loose and his body fell into the river, and he would have been drowned had it not been for his faithful old colored servant (Uncle Abram Robb) who, holding his arms, pulled him into the boat. He died at his home February 17, 1862."

"The spirit of the boys would not permit them to remain at home"

Polk G. Johnson, a student at Stewart College in the last days before the Civil War, wrote in 1885 about those troubled times:

"Just before the war the people of Montgomery county were almost unanimously in favor of preserving the Federal Union; but when President Lincoln called for troops to subdue the South, there was a complete revolution in public feeling. At the election held for 'separation' or 'no separation,' they were almost unanimous. The spirit of the people was high. Every man able to speak spoke in opposition to the proclamation of the President, and advised resistance.

"The spirit of the boys would not permit them to remain at home. No longer were groups of boys in the College, earnest in their studies, to be seen under the shade of the old oaks in the College campus, engaged with their books; no longer they idle in gay conversation upon the steps of the College. The whole scene was changed. Books were thrown away, and the grounds became a *champ de mars*. The tramp of the soldier, the commands of the officer (Prof. W. A. Forbes) were alone to be seen or heard upon the grounds or in the halls; and the same spirit animated all the boys not in college. No wonder, then, that they made such a prompt response to the call.

"Of thirty-two boys in the College Department of its last catalog of 1859-60, twenty-nine entered the Confederate army, leaving but three who did not. Of this twenty-nine all were faithful. There were killed in battle, sixteen; died by disease, seven; total deaths, twenty-three; survivors, six."

One of the six survivors, of course, was Mr. Johnson. He was wounded several times, had his horse shot from under him in the battle of Lick-Skillet Road at Atlanta, and was surrendered with Lee's army at Appomattox. He returned to Clarksville, then attended McGill College in Montreal and Cumberland University in Lebanon, Tennessee, for his legal education. He was a successful lawyer in Clarksville and for many years served as Clerk and Master of the Chancery Court. His first wife, who died after only three years of marriage, was Emma Robb, daughter of Col. Alfred Robb.

After the War

Among the many casualties of the war was President McMullen. During the occupation of Clarksville, an outbreak of smallpox afflicted many of the federal soldiers. His humanity rising above his dislike of the invaders, McMullen worked as a nurse in the hospital set up by the army in Robb Hall, contracted the disease himself, and died of it in January 1865.

The sad condition of the campus and the devastated Southern economic system made getting the College back on its feet a long and painful project. At one point the trustees were so disheartened by the difficulties that they recommended to the Synod of Nashville that the property be sold to another institution. But in April 1869, a final fundraising push by the Synod resulted in enough money to repair the buildings and reopen the school.

With former President William Stewart serving as Acting President, classes resumed in September 1869. A total of seventy students were enrolled.

When the 1870-71 session opened, enrollment had risen to a healthy 101 students, and a new President was in the chair. Rev. J.B. Shearer, a graduate of the University of Virginia and Union Seminary, brought with him some positive ideas about the development of the Christian college. Under his guidance the curriculum was revised to offer more electives, high standards of scholarship were promoted, and the securing of great teachers at any cost became an even higher priority.

President Shearer also devoted himself to procuring a wider base of support for the College. He envisioned "one grand University for the whole church South, to be under the care of the Presbyterian people."

New President John Shearer and former President William Stewart are pictured at the top of this photocomposite of the school and its faculty in the early 1870s.

His vision was realized in early 1874, when the Synods of Alabama, Arkansas, Memphis, Mississippi/Louisiana, Nashville (and later Texas) adopted a Plan of Union for the support of a Presbyterian university. Later that year, a committee to select the site for this new university heard proposals from Huntsville and Opelika, Alabama; Meridian, Mississippi; and Bolivar, Jackson, and Clarksville, Tennessee. Memphis was briefly discussed, but the recent yellow fever epidemic there removed that city from the running. Clarksville, with its Stewart College facility and a pledge of $50,000, won the day.

STEWART COLLEGE.

Clarksville, Tenn.

Rev. JAMES A. LYON, D. D.,
President elect, and Prof. of Ethics, Metaphysics, Logic, etc.

W. M. STEWART, A. M.,
Physical Sciences.

Rev. D. OWEN DAVIES, A. M.,
Rhetoric and the Belles Lettres.

Mathematics.

To be supplied at the August meeting of of the Board.

Greek and Latin.

The duties of this Chair will be discharged by other members of the Faculty until the appointment of a Professor.

Prof. D. M. QUARLES, A. M.,
Principal Preparatory Department and Professor of Modern Languages.

Expenses, per Session of 20 Weeks.
Tuition, Collegiate $35.00
"   Classical 30.00
"   English Preparatory 25.00
Modern Languages, each 10.00
Contingent Fee 2.00
Board (including room, fire, etc.,)
   per month . . . . $15 to 20
Session begins on the first Monday in September.   July 15

This advertisement appeared July 15, 1869, in the Clarksville Leaf-Chronicle. Although Rev. James A. Lyon had accepted the Board's offer of the presidency, his church in Columbus, Mississippi, strongly resisted his departure. So when school opened in September, former President Stewart assumed the role of Acting President.

Southwestern Presbyterian University

For various reasons, chiefly financial, Stewart College did not become Southwestern Presbyterian University until five years later, in 1879. President Shearer spent much of his tenure on the road, at the request of the Synods, attempting to raise money for the new University. But the financial condition of the country after the panic of 1873 made fundraising a frustrating and exhausting task. However, during that time, enrollment and faculty continued to increase, as did the physical plant. A major new building, completed in 1878, was named in honor of the recently deceased William Stewart, who had given so much of himself to the College.

One of the leading advocates of the University in the Presbyterian Church, Dr. Benjamin M. Palmer, pastor of the First Presbyterian Church in New Orleans, was asked to take on the presidency of the College. He accepted, but his church and the Presbytery of New Orleans resisted his departure so strongly that he withdrew his acceptance. Dr. Palmer remained a close friend and supporter of the College for the rest of his life, and authored the section of the Plan of Union that removed the University from the direct management of the Synods and provided that "the sole government of the institution shall be in the hands of a directory, consisting of two members from each Synod, one elected each year after the first."

By 1879, the financial difficulties of the mid-1870s had eased somewhat, and the University was officially opened, with a new title—Chancellor—for the man at its helm, and a new man to fill the position, Dr. J.N. Waddel.

Like his immediate predecessors

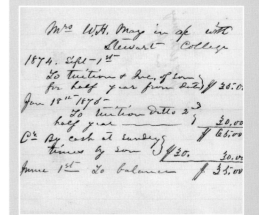

This invoice was sent to parents in 1874 for the education of their son at the College. The $35-per-term cost was constant through the '70s, dropped to $25 per term in the '80s, and rose to $30 in the '90s.

In 1886 the faculty and student body of SPU gather on the steps of the Castle for a portrait with top hats and bowlers in hand. The splendid white side-whiskers in the front row (third from right) belong to the highly esteemed Chancellor J.N. Waddel.

McMullen and Shearer, Waddel was a Presbyterian minister. He had also served as Chancellor of the University of Mississippi in the years following the end of the Civil War, and at the present time was

The Waddel Building, 1899

serving as secretary of the Board of Education of the Southern Presbyterian Church.

With the support of the Synods behind it, the University once more seemed to have been given a new lease on life. Although it would never be completely free of financial worries, the school now entered upon an era of relative strength and stability. Now it could truly concentrate

its efforts on its educational mission.

Morale was so much improved that the editor of the Clarksville *Chronicle* took note of it on a visit to the campus. "A very satisfactory change is observable. The students now present the unmistakable appearance of young men who have plenty to do and are doing it. The lounging, listless expression hitherto observable is altogether thrown off, and such a thing as a student loafing on street corners is not to be seen."

Among Dr. Waddel's innovations was one dear to his heart, the establishment of a School of Theology. Again, Dr. B.M. Palmer came to the aid of the school with his encouragement and assistance. The women of his church in New Orleans helped raise the money to endow the chair of Theology, which was named the Palmer Professorship of Theology.

The first occupant of that chair was the distinguished preacher and religious scholar, Dr. Joseph R. Wilson, who inaugurated the new theology school in 1885. Dr. Wilson, whose elder son Woodrow would later become President of the United States, remained at the head of the theology school until his retirement in 1892.

During the 1870s and '80s, campus life expanded beyond the classroom to encompass a much wider range of social and athletic activities. The two debating societies that had been established before the war continued to provide intellectual stimulation and frequent oratorical contests. But now the first fraternities were established. Backlot games turned into organized athletic programs. Glee clubs and marching bands appeared.

Ill health forced Dr. Waddel to retire as Chancellor in 1888. He was replaced, briefly, by Dr. C.C. Hersman, who returned to his native South Carolina after three years, and then by Dr. J.M. Rawlings, who lasted barely a year before a severe illness caused him to withdraw.

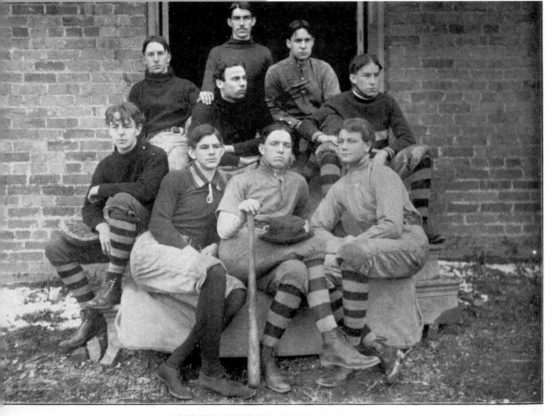

'VARSITY BASEBALL TEAM OF '98

PRICE   ORR   ALBRIGHT   RAWORTH
PIPES   MCLAIN   COX   BARTON   NORWOOD

Dr. George Summey, the managing editor of the *Presbyterian Quarterly Review*, accepted the chancellorship in 1892 and served for the next ten years. Despite continuing budget problems, Summey managed to add to the campus by completing the Waddel Building (an attachment to the Stewart Building that included a gymnasium); and by building a new dormitory, Calvin Hall.

Summey's energetic efforts throughout the Synods to increase the endowment yielded such disappointing results that he resigned in 1902, declaring that "the burden is greater, in some respects, than I can bear, and I cannot continue to undertake it."

After Summey's ten-year tenure, the University was headed by a succession of five different men over the next fifteen years. Each in his own way struggled with the enormous problems of carrying out the educational mission of the school in spite of dwindling financial support. During these years, enrollment swung erratically from a high of 135 to a low of 74.

In 1903, the Board of the University also had to contend with a movement, largely on the part of the city of Atlanta, to transfer the University to a large city where it might more easily attract the attention of wealthier donors. The Board appealed to the Supreme Court of Tennessee for protection and in 1904 received a judgment in their favor, expressly banning a move to any other state, and decreeing that the "said institution must be maintained at Clarksville, Montgomery County, Tennessee."

But the idea—that to save the school it must be moved—could not be decreed away. There was a feeling throughout the Synods that the Clarksville location at the northern edge of the Synods' territory was partly responsible for some of its problems.

Accordingly, when Dr. Charles E. Diehl, pastor of the First Presbyterian Church in Clarksville, was approached by a committee from the Board and offered the presidency of the University (the title "chancellor" had by then been dropped), the subject of its possible removal was discussed. At that time, Dr. Diehl was convinced that there was no legal way this could be done, so he accepted the presidency with the thought that his challenge was to enlarge the scope of the University within its Clarksville parameters.

But by 1919, he had changed his mind. Loyal to the city of Clarksville, but even more loyal to the needs of the church and of the institution he now headed, he was convinced that the school's salvation demanded that it be moved.

When Dr. M.E. Melvin, a member of the Board, came to his fellow directors in June of 1919 with an offer to raise $1,000,000 for the University if it would move to Memphis, the Board accepted his proposal. In January of 1920, this proposal was put before a meeting of the Synods in Nashville, to the great consternation of the civic leaders of Clarksville.

Unfortunately for Clarksville, the die was cast. The Board began legal proceedings to negate the 1904 decree. Fundraising campaigns were initiated in Memphis and throughout the Synods. Dr. Diehl talked to architects.

As soon as the Board had enough money and pledges in hand to pay for the first building, the College began construction in Memphis—gambling that the legal problems would be resolved. On March 8, 1924, the State Supreme Court decided in favor of the University. On September 24, 1925, classes began on the new campus in Memphis, with yet another new name.

Women were admitted to SPU on the same terms as men in 1917. In 1921, Margaret Elwyn Trahern became the first woman to receive a degree from the College. She was a member of the honor society, a charter member of Chi Omega sorority, and a member of Kappa Delta Literary Society. She was married to William Green Patch of Clarksville in 1925.

The Castle:
"stately, elegant, capacious and imposing."

"The site of the College edifice . . . is about a half mile back from the river, on a beautiful and elevated lot of ground, containing about six acres. The building was designed by Prof. J.H. Ingraham, and having been adopted by the trustees, was placed in the hands of Mr. Briscoe Vannoy, a young and promising architect of this city (Nashville), who drew the front and the ground plan on a large scale with the details."
—From the reports of Wilkins Tannehill, head of the Masonic Lodges of Tennessee, March 1849

The Clarksville *Jeffersonian* enthusiastically welcomed the new building in 1850: "What an elegant structure it is! Of vast extent and built in the handsomest style of Elizabethan architecture, it arrests the attention of every passerby, no matter were he from Rome, that city of St. Peter's Cathedral."

When the SPU grounds and buildings were reincarnated as the site of Austin Peay State College in 1929, the Castle served as that school's administration building. The collapsing of one of the towers in 1948 necessitated the demolition of the ninety-eight-year-old structure.

As Stewart College metamorphosed into Southwestern Presbyterian University, the increased enrollment and expanded curriculum called for more classroom space. Accordingly, early in 1877 a new building was begun. Called at first the Cabinet Building, its name was changed to the Stewart Building after the death in September 1877 of Prof. William M. Stewart, who had given so generously of his fortune and his services to the College. Construction expenses for the new building were recorded in a journal and summarized on the pages shown at right.

The Castle
The College's first building, completed in June 1850 at a cost of $32,000.

Waddel Hall
Barely visible behind Stewart Hall, to which it is attached, Waddel was built in 1899 and contained an assembly hall and the gymnasium.

The Stewart Building

The bell that hung in the tower of the Stewart Building was rung to summon students to classes throughout the day. When the College moved to Memphis the bell was brought along and installed in an arch created for it in Neely Hall, where it still hangs today.

Robb Hall, the first dormitory

Born in Sumner County, Tennessee, Alfred Robb settled in Clarksville in 1850 and soon became one of its most respected lawyers. He was a strong supporter of Stewart College and a member of the Board of Trustees. His enthusiasm for the college led Robb to donate a valuable piece of land adjacent to it for the purpose of building a dormitory so that the school could atract more "foreign" students from neighboring counties and states. Thus the College's first dormitory was called Robb Hall.

Completed just a year before the Civil War, Robb Hall served only briefly as a dormitory before it was turned into a hospital, first for Confederate soldiers, later for federals. It resumed its proper function when the College reopened in 1869 and continued as such until the College removed to Memphis. At Austin Peay, it remained a dormitory until the mid-1960s, when it was razed to make space for a new building.

The Commons
This dining hall, built in 1918, was the last building erected on the campus before the move to Memphis. It also served as a meeting place for both student and community organizations.

Calvin Hall
The second men's dormitory was added in 1895.

Robb Hall

"From now on I will fight you to the limit."

REMOVAL OF S. P. U. TO MEMPHIS IS FAVORED BY TENNESSEE SYNOD

Trustees Are Authorized to Take Such Legal Action as May be Necessary to Transfer Institution if They Deem Advisable.

Clarksville Delegation of 45 Men Make Eloquent Appeals for Retention of School Here—Short History of University—Alabama Also Favors Removal.

SHIPPING FRAUD OF A BILLION

BIG PACIFIC COAST CONCERNS FACE PROSECUTION BY GOVERNMENT.

When Dr. Diehl agreed to the proposal to move the College to Memphis, he knew it would cause a considerable change in his life. There was an enormous amount of work to be done in raising the money for the new facility, in actually getting it built, and in the physical move itself.

There would also be enormous resistance to the move from the residents of Clarksville, who were justly proud of their many contributions to the College over the past seven decades. So Dr. Diehl fully expected a somewhat hostile reaction from his neighbors.

"Even in the Rotary Club, of which I was a charter member, there was ill-concealed coldness. The man who served as best man in my wedding was quite frank in his attitude. He said, 'Diehl, up to this time we have been warm friends, but from now on I will fight you to the limit.' On one occasion, shortly after this attitude became so evident, I made a talk at the Rotary Club, reminding the members that as pastor of the First Presbyterian Church my first obligation was to that church and to Clarksville, but that when I became President of Southwestern, which was owned and controlled by four Synods of the Presbyterian Church in the United States, my first obligation was not to Clarksville but to the four Synods whose institution Southwestern is. I also reminded them that there was no change in my relationship to the people of Clarksville, and that I was as devoted to them as I had always been. I offered to resign from the Rotary Club if that were the desire of the Club. My remarks seemed to ease the situation a bit, and I did not resign as a member of the Club. However, Mrs. Diehl and I were made to feel that in many cases the old relationship had been greatly affected. She was not well and was accustomed to sit on the lovely porch of the President's house, which was the best house either of us had ever lived in, but her friends did not stop by to visit with her as they had done before my attitude toward the proposed removal became known."

Piomingo College? Calvin College? Southminster College? Renaming the College, the 1921 Version

Once the decision had been made to move the College to Memphis, Dr. Diehl and the Board discussed changing the name. With the Board's concurrence, Dr. Diehl first proposed "Memphis College." Ever a practical man, he noted that such a name would have "the best appeal locally, and will get us more money where the money will have to be gotten."

Chief fundraiser Dr. M.E. Melvin, who had been instrumental in initiating the move to Memphis, did not agree. He felt it would hurt appeals to alumni. An Indian name, he suggested, might be more palatable. After conferring with Judge J.H. Malone of Memphis, "the greatest living authority" on the Chickasaw Nation, Melvin proposed the name of the great chief of the Chickasaws and friend of George Washington, Piomingo, which means Mountain Leader.

Dr. Diehl's reaction was terse. "Piomingo is impossible—I would say it is ungodly."

And so the search continued. Among the rejects: Calvin College, Southminster College, Gayoso College, Chisca College, and Al-La-Mis-Ten College.

When the dust settled and the move was complete, the letterhead of the College read simply *Southwestern, The College of the Mississippi Valley*, a name that would satisfy both the alumni and the donors in Memphis. Most important, according to Dr. Diehl, "it would distinguish it from that little two by four institution in Kansas."

> ## NOT SATISFIED WITH THE NAME
>
> The Board of Directors of S. P. U. are not altogether satisfied with the name "Memphis College," which they have tentatively and recently chosen. The choice of a name presents a real difficulty. The word "University" must be eliminated.
>
> Constructive suggestions from the Alumni are invited. We should speak now or forever hold our peace.
>
> The drift of sentiment now seems to be for this: "Southwestern College at Memphis, Tennessee," which would find a parallel in "Tulane University of Louisiana."
>
> Write immediately to President C. E. Diehl, Clarksville, Tenn., if you have any sentiment to express. We ought to at least retain the name "Southwestern."
>
> M. E. MELVIN,
> Campaign Manager.
> (Class 1900)

A bulletin to the alumni announcing the name change to Memphis College drew a flood of alumni objections—and some interesting suggestions.

This aerial photo shows the Memphis campus from the air in the late 1920s: Palmer Hall is on the left, and the wooden Fargason Field House is on the right.

Southwestern

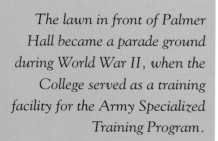

-THREE SENIORS GI

CTS Southwestern Seniors Scatter to Four
ORS Corners of Earth; Jobs are Too Scarce

Many Graduate Without Definite Plans For Future;
Teaching and Further Study Most Popular

A survey of the plans of Southwestern's seniors for the coming year
shows that many of them are uncertain about their futures. Four boys,
Perry Bynum, Joe C. Mobley and John and James Hughes, will enter the
University of Tennessee Medical College in September. John Hughes and
Perry Bynum will spend the summer as assistant directors in boys' camps,
and James Hughes will go to Little Rock, Ark., to work during vacation
as an orderly in the Arkansas State

The Sou'wester, May 27, 1932

*Lorenzo Childress, Jr. '69 was
the College's first black graduate.*

*The lawn in front of Palmer
Hall became a parade ground
during World War II, when the
College served as a training
facility for the Army Specialized
Training Program.*

The move to Memphis did not solve all the College's problems, but it invigorated the institution to such an extent that those problems no longer seemed solution-resistant. One cause for this optimism: enrollment at the last Clarksville session had been 187; the first Memphis session had 406 students.

The College opened in Memphis with a mortgage of $700,000. Within only five years that entire debt had been paid in full, and a joyous mortgage-burning was held on July 1, 1930.

The Great Depression took its toll on enrollment, as fewer and fewer families could afford to send their children to college. Faculty salaries were reduced, expenses were pared whenever possible, but the torch of knowledge never wavered. By 1935 enrollment had started to climb again, this time passing the 500 mark for the first time in the school's history. In 1937 Dr. Diehl bravely proposed a $3,500,000 building plan to include dormitories, a library, a gymnasium, and a student center. But in 1941, once again, war put the College's growth plans on the shelf.

When the war was ended in 1945, Dr. Diehl launched the Southwestern Pre-Centennial Endowment Fund campaign and successfully raised $2,500,000. New buildings began to rise around the campus.

Dr. Diehl announced his decision to retire in 1947, and the timing of the school's centennial celebration was adjusted to coincide with the installation of his successor. Consequently, September of 1949 brought to the campus a double ceremony—the Centennial Commemoration and the Inaugural Celebration of Dr. Peyton N. Rhodes as the new President.

Under Dr. Rhodes, the College continued to grow, with a steady increase in enrollment and an almost continuous construction process on the campus. When he retired in 1965, ten new buildings graced the campus, and enrollment had grown from 600 to 900 students a year.

To replace Dr. Rhodes, the Board chose a young alumnus of the College, Dr. John David Alexander, who brought vigor, imagination and a host of fresh ideas to the curriculum in the brief four years he spent on the campus before leaving for Pomona College in California. His successor, Dr. William L. Bowden, another alumnus of the College, concentrated his efforts on increasing administrative efficiency and strengthening ties with the Memphis community. He resigned in 1972 to serve the Southern Governor's Conference.

A short reign,
but a busy one:
John David Alexander

He was, at the time, one of the youngest sitting presidents of an American college.

He was also the first elected President of this College to have earned his undergraduate degree here. Only eleven years after receiving his B.A., thirty-three-year-old John David Alexander returned in triumph to become the sixteenth chief executive of his alma mater on July 1, 1965.

Those eleven years had been productive ones: further study at Louisville Theological Seminary; a Rhodes Scholarship to Oxford, where he received his D. Phil. degree from Christ Church; marriage to his college sweetheart, Catherine Ballard Coleman; ordination as a Presbyterian minister; and seven years teaching the Old Testament at San Francisco Theological Seminary.

Obviously a man of energy and ideas, Alexander plunged immediately into the formidable project of reviewing and renovating all aspects of the College's educational system. Working closely with a task force of representatives from the faculty, students, and administration, he achieved within two years an almost complete overhaul of the academic program.

Alexander's calm but firm controlling hand kept the College on course during the rebellious late '60s, an era that saw many established dress and behavior guidelines modified or eliminated with minimal stress and disorder.

The College community was shocked and chagrined when, in January 1969, Alexander announced that he was resigning to become President of Pomona College. *The Commercial Appeal* expressed the feeling of many when it editorialized:

"Dr. David Alexander's tenure has been brief, but he has left his mark. He has in three short years caused a ferment of ideas. He has helped raise the level of conscience of the entire Memphis community. He has created new areas of understanding between different age groups. He has been a major contributor to better race relations. In short, he has performed in the tradition of the liberal arts scholar."

Alexander returned to Rhodes in 1986 to accept the Doctor of Letters honorary degree.

Rhodes College

The budget deficit that had so concerned Dr. Bowden darkened the horizon for the new President as well. But Dr. James H. Daughdrill, Jr. came to the job with a particular set of talents that suited him well for the task ahead. He had been a successful businessman, a Presbyterian minister, and Secretary of Stewardship for the Presbyterian Church, U.S. Within his first year he had erased the deficit, and, for the last twenty-four years, he has kept the College deficit-free. In the tenth year of his tenure, he boldly agreed to a proposal to change the name of the College yet again.

Dr. Daughdrill has also managed to propel the building program, with eight new additions to the campus. He has supervised the growth of the endowment, that Holy Grail of so many past presidents, from $6 million in 1973 to $207 million in 1998.

But most important, he has seen this College recognized as "the No. 1 Up-and-Coming College in the Nation" by *U.S. News and World Report*; as one of "The Best, Most Popular and Most Exciting Colleges in the United States" by *Barron's*; and as one of "the Thirty-Six Character-Building Colleges" in the nation by the Templeton Foundation.

The visionary words of Thomas Elliott as he stood before the first building of this College—"I am looking at a perpetuity"— now seem truly prophetic. For this institution stands at the end of its first 150 years on firmer ground than at any time in its frequently troubled past. Rhodes College approaches the twenty-first century with pride in its past and justified optimism for its future.

Surely the spirits of all those who worked so tirelessly for the last century and a half to sustain and nourish this place must be rejoicing today—as should all who love this College.

Roster of Presidents

Presidents of Masonic University of Tennessee:
W.F. Hopkins, 1848-49
Richard Nelson Newell, A.M., 1849-50
Presidents of Montgomery Masonic College:
William A. Forbes, A.M., 1850-53
William M. Stewart, 1853-55
Presidents of Stewart College:
William M. Stewart, 1855-58
R.B. McMullen, D.D., 1859-62
William M. Stewart, 1869-70 (Acting)
J.B. Shearer, A.M., D.D., 1870-79
Chancellors of Southwestern Presbyterian University:
John N. Waddel, D.D., LL.D., 1879-88
Charles C. Hersman, D.D., 1888-91
James M. Rawlings, D.D., 1891-92
George Summey, D.D., 1892-1903
George F. Nicolassen, A.M., LL.D., 1903-05 (Acting)
Neander M. Woods, D.D., LL.D., 1905-08
William Dinwiddie, A.M., LL.D., 1908-14
Presidents of Southwestern Presbyterian University:
John R. Dobyns, LL.D., 1914-17
George Lang, M.A., D.D., (Acting from Jan. 1917-June 1917)
Charles E. Diehl, A.M., D.D., 1917-25
President of Southwestern:
Charles E. Diehl, A.M, D.D., LL.D., 1925-49
Presidents of Southwestern at Memphis:
Peyton Nalle Rhodes, A.M., Ph.D., 1949-65
John David Alexander, B.A., Ph.D., 1965-69
William Lukens Bowden, B.A., M.A., Ph.D., 1969-73
James Harold Daughdrill, Jr., B.A., M. Div., D.D., 1973-
President of Rhodes College:
James Harold Daughdrill, Jr., B.A., M. Div., D.D., 1973-

Carved in Stone:
Changing the Name, 1984 Version

The urge to discard the inappropriate Southwestern part of the College's name had been around ever since the move to Memphis, as witness the Board's considerations at that time.

When the matter arose again in 1984, several months of research and intense, not to say heated, discussion ensued. All elements of the College community were invited to participate in the process—alumni, students, faculty, and friends. Comments and suggestions were solicited, then the responses were reviewed by a committee, representing the various constituencies, who made a recommendation to the Board.

When Board chairman Frank M. Mitchener announced that the College was to be named in honor of former President Peyton Nalle Rhodes, he said, "By their action the Trustees have chosen to link the spirit of this College with the inspiration of the man who has helped to give it life for over half a century."

Dr. Rhodes joined the College as Associate Professor of Physics in 1926, and soon thereafter became a full professor. In 1944, he was named Vice-President and in 1949, President, serving until his retirement in 1965. Even in retirement he continued to serve the College when needed: as acting President, acting Vice-President, acting Dean, and as building consultant.

"Dr. Rhodes embodies the values on which this institution was founded," said President James H. Daughdrill, Jr. "His relentless crusade for excellence, his belief in liberal education, and his unfailing love for the College make it altogether fitting that this institution be named in his honor. Much of what exists at the College today is the result of Dr. Rhodes' vision and leadership."

Heading to class on an autumn day, Marty Newcomb '98 (left), Dave Harrison '97 (center), and Bryan Smith '98 make their way through the arch between Robinson and Williford Halls.

This desk was built in the 1920s for Dr. Charles E. Diehl's office in Palmer Hall. It has been used by each president of the College since. The matching computer return and the brass label inside a drawer were added by President James Daughdrill, Jr.

Chapter Two: The Presidents of the College

In one of his *First Essays*, Ralph Waldo Emerson wrote, "An institution is but the lengthened shadow of a man."

And beyond all doubt, the 150-year history of this institution must be seen as the long shadows of several great men. Surely a benevolent Being watched over this school and sent to it, at the times they were needed most, a series of leaders who preserved it, nourished it, and shaped it into what it is today. Of special note are six leaders of this college, three from the nineteenth century and three from the twentieth, whose efforts kept this institution alive or substantially changed its path for the better.

As different as they were, these men shared a commonality of vision, determination and dedication to Christian education. Without them, there is a strong likelihood this college would not now exist, certainly not in the way that we know it.

"It is not given to many men to know that they belong to history."

—Rev. Benjamin M. Palmer, speaking at the unveiling of a portrait of Chancellor John N. Waddel, June 1888

William May Stewart: Principal Friend and Pilot

President, 1853-58
Acting President, 1869-70

Although much of the acclaimed Vanuxem collection of minerals was destroyed by the Union soldiers who occupied the Castle during the Civil War, some were saved. They are now displayed in the Frazier Jelke Science Center.

According to contemporary reports, he was a soft-spoken, modest man: "The subdued cheerfulness and high-bred courtesy of his manner made it as delightful as it was profitable . . . He had the grace of Chesterfield without his chill, the heartiness of the Western man without his roughness."

William Stewart was born in Philadelphia in March 1803. Fascinated from an early age by the phenomena of the natural world, at ten years old he was devoting his spare time to observing and collecting insects and shellfish. When he was twenty, he was invited to become a member of Philadelphia's prestigious Academy of Natural Sciences. Later he put his scientific knowledge to profitable use when he moved to the iron-rich region of middle Tennessee in 1832 and became a very successful manufacturer of pig iron.

When the Masonic orders of Tennessee decided to turn the Clarksville Academy into a college, Stewart was one of eight men who underwrote the construction costs for the College's first building, the Castle. Most of these donors, like Stewart, had made fortunes in the iron business. In appreciation for their generosity, the trustees incised their names in a marble tablet embedded in the red brick above the main entrance of the Castle. That tablet can now be seen on the south face of the Richard Halliburton Memorial Tower.

This contribution was to be only the first of many that Stewart would make.

When the College opened its session of 1851-52, Stewart, now retired from his iron factory, was listed on the faculty roster as Professor of Natural Sciences. What the roster does not note is that he was serving without remuneration, which he continued to do throughout his connection with the College.

In 1853, Stewart accepted an invitation to serve as President of the College. When the Nashville Synod assumed ownership of the school in 1855, its leadership resolved: "That in consequence of the munificent donations, of long continued and disinterested service, of ardent and untiring devotion to science, and of the high Christian and moral character of Wm. M. Stewart, the President of said Institution, that it be called in his honor, 'Stewart College.' "

Among the "munificent donations" Stewart had made to the College was the Vanuxem collection, a famous and extensive collection of 6,000 mineral specimens and 16,000 fossils, described as "the largest, finest, and most systematically arranged private collection in the United States."

Stewart, the serious scholar and generous giver, was unfortunately not the bush-beating fundraiser the young College needed most in its presidential chair. In 1858 he resigned his presidential duties and helped the trustees secure the services of Rev. R.B. McMullen to take over the leadership of the College. And when McMullen conducted a drive to create an endowment for the College, Stewart was one of the major contributors.

After the Civil War, with the Castle stripped to its bare walls and floors by the Union soldiers and the refugees who had later been quartered there, it was Stewart, now as Chairman of the Board of

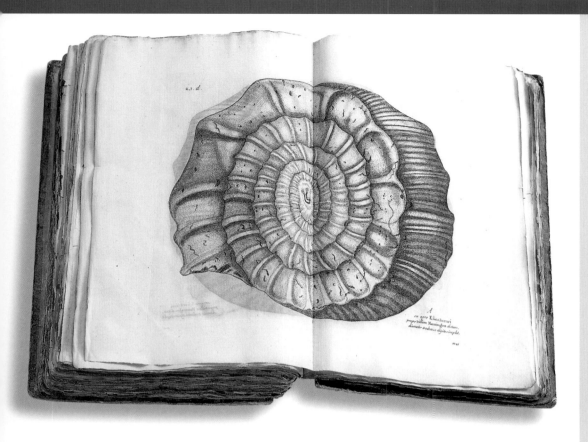

These rare seventeenth-century French drawings of shellfish are another of Stewart's gifts to the College.

Trustees, who had the duty of reporting to the Synod of Nashville the sad condition of the College. Without a substantial amount of money for repairs, he concluded, the College could not be reopened. When the money was miraculously raised, it was Stewart who once again served as Acting President in the first session until the newly elected John Shearer could arrive to take charge.

From about 1852 and continuing almost up until his death in 1877, Stewart maintained a collaboration with the Smithsonian Institution, using his own instruments to record local weather conditions. At the urging of the Smithsonian's curator, Stewart also arranged collections of Tennessee reptiles, fish, and small mammals for the museum. His personal collection of shells from all over the world numbered more than 17,000 and included hundreds of bivalves from Tennessee rivers, all properly identified and cataloged.

When Stewart died, his faculty colleagues saluted "the purity of his life, the gentleness of his manners, the modesty and childlike simplicity which characterized

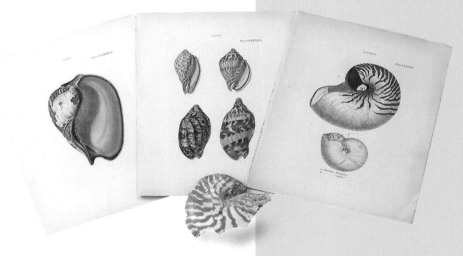

his discourse with everyone, the frank and generous bearing which he always displayed in every relation."

It is in these last qualities that Stewart left his most valuable legacy. His honesty, his lack of pretension, and his dedication to learning established a tradition of genuineness and concern for academic excellence that has continued to shape the course of this college ever since.

A number of the scientific texts donated to the College by Stewart are kept in the Rare Book Room of the Burrow Library.

John Bunyan Shearer: A Hero from Virginia

President, 1870-79

If William Stewart was the first savior of the College, then surely Rev. John Bunyan Shearer was its second. Born and educated in Virginia, he received his undergraduate degree from Hampden-Sydney College, his Master's from the University of Virginia, and his divinity degree from Union Seminary at Hampden-Sydney. Ordained as a minister in 1858, his first pastorate was at Chapel Hill, North Carolina, which he served until the Civil War halted the activities of the University of North Carolina. After the war he served several churches and taught at a private school in Halifax County, Virginia.

When he arrived at Stewart College in 1870, he faced a daunting task. The devastation of the region's economy by the war and Reconstruction made fundraising well-nigh impossible. The Nashville

After Shearer's wedding to Miss Lizzie Gessner of Prince Edward County, Virginia, the solemn couple sat for this daguerreotype portrait.

Synod was able to keep the College functioning, but with no increase in the meager endowment, there was little chance for the school to prosper. Shearer spent so much of his time in the thankless job of trying to find money for the College that the Board granted him an assistant to manage the school's day-to-day activities.

But if Shearer's financial efforts were not as successful as he would have liked, he more than compensated by making two significant and enduring contributions to the future of the institution.

First, he reorganized the curriculum along the lines of that of his alma mater, the University of Virginia. Following the guidelines of that school's founder, Thomas Jefferson, he set forth five goals: the recognition of real university standards of instruction and scholarship; the establishment of distinct "schools" in which great subjects were grouped; the securing of great teachers at any cost; the creation of an elective system, departing from the prescribed classical formula formerly offered; and the establishment of a course of study in the Bible.

Second, realizing that a school of the scope and quality he envisioned was beyond the resources of the Nashville Synod, Shearer joined with Dr. J.A. Lyon and Dr. B.M. Palmer to promote to the Synods of the Southwest the Plan of Union that ultimately resulted in the conversion of Stewart College into Southwestern Presbyterian University in 1879.

Exhausted from raising funds, Shearer was happy to relinquish leadership of the new University to Dr. J.N. Waddel and limit his role to teaching. He remained at the College as Professor of Biblical Studies, Hebrew, and New Testament Greek until 1888, when he was elected to the presidency of Davidson College in North Carolina. He retired as President in 1901, continuing to serve as Vice-President until his death in 1918. He is remembered at Davidson for his strong mind, his generosity to needy students, and, alas, his long prayers, as Mary D. Beaty observed in her history of Davidson: "Thirty minute prayers were as nothing to him; a congregation, standing when he began, would all be collapsed in pews when he reached the 'amen'."

Rev. J.N. Waddel: The First Chancellor

Chancellor, 1879-88

When the Synods of the Southwest took over Stewart College and converted it to Southwestern Presbyterian University in 1879, they wisely chose Dr. John N. Waddel to serve as Chancellor (a new title for the presiding officer of the institution, based upon its new status as a university).

Dr. Waddel's experience and talents were exactly what the reborn school needed. Born in 1812 in Willington, South Carolina, he was the son of an eminent Presbyterian minister and educator, Dr. Moses Waddel, who served as President of the University of Georgia from 1819-29. After graduating from his father's school, John Waddel followed his distinguished father's footsteps, first as a teacher, then as a minister.

In 1841, he moved to Mississippi with his brother-in-law, Dr. J.H. Gray, with whom Waddel founded Montrose Academy and several churches. In 1848, when the new University of Mississippi opened its doors in Oxford, he was a member of its faculty, serving as Professor of Greek and Latin.

In his *Memorials of Academic Life*, Dr. Waddel described the first class of Ole Miss students in despairing terms: "In point of morals and habits of application to duty, and intellectual advancement, the large body of the students were idle, uncultivated, viciously disposed, and ungovernable ... In my opinion nothing saved the University from utter and speedy ruin, under God's blessing, but the sternest and most rigid exercise of discipline."

Dr. Waddel was present at the birth of yet another college in 1857 when he joined the faculty of LaGrange Synodical College just outside Memphis, where his brother-in-law Dr. Gray was now president. Like Stewart College, LaGrange was founded by an alliance between a Presbyterian Synod (that of Memphis) and the Masonic lodges of that region. After only three years in the presidency, Dr. Gray resigned, and Dr. Waddel was prevailed upon to take over the reins of the school in 1860.

Again like Stewart College, LaGrange College was occupied by Federal troops during the Civil War. But instead of being merely vandalized, it was completely destroyed—LaGrange's buildings were leveled and its bricks used to build huts for the Union soldiers.

Waddel himself was at one point in danger of imprisonment for refusing to sign an oath of loyalty to the U.S. government, but he managed to slip through enemy lines at night and escape to join the Army of the Mississippi as commissioner in charge of chaplains.

When the University of Mississippi reopened after the war, Waddel was called to its chancellorship, and over the next nine years managed to get the struggling institution back on its feet. He left in 1874 to serve as Secretary of Education for the Presbyterian Churches of the South and spent most of his time traveling through the Synods and attempting to raise money for the proposed new Southwestern Presbyterian University.

So it seemed logical and right that when the new school officially opened its first session in September 1879, its Chancellor was John N. Waddel.

His scholarship, religious credentials, administrative ability, invaluable experience with taming the "ungovernable" Ole Miss students, and his popularity throughout the Synods of the Southwest combined to make him the ideal leader for SPU, as the revitalized institution soon came to be known. He was loved and respected by students and faculty alike, and was greatly missed when he retired in 1888. He died in 1895.

The LaGrange Synodical College under Union occupation. Harper's Weekly, *Dec. 20, 1862, engraving by A. Simplot.*

Party Politics: Why Waddel Left Ole Miss, June 24, 1874

As Chancellor of a state university, Waddel was subject to the usual pressures of political appointees. During Reconstruction, it was particularly difficult for longtime Southerners to stomach the arrogance of the Republican carpetbaggers and scalawags in state government. He explains his final decision to resign from the chancellorship as a social and political conflict:

"At the Chancellor's annual reception during Commencement week, the Trustees were present, and among them those who belonged to the Republican party. As I sincerely desired to have them feel at home and enjoy the evening, I made it a point that ought to be observed, to have those gentlemen introduced to the ladies who were present. I, at the same time, took the precaution to ascertain the personal sentiment of the ladies in this regard, and ascertain whether it would be agreeable to them to be presented in this way, and this I did without the slightest intimation to the Trustees themselves. Every lady whom I approached declined very quietly, but very promptly. These gentlemen (I was informed by a party present in company with them) resented this neglect, and laid the entire blame to my charge, considering it a tacit purpose on my part, and a practical indignity done to themselves. It was just one of those unavoidable occurrences one is called to encounter sometimes in society, which could not be explained without making matters worse; so I said nothing to anyone about it. But as I heard of the fact as stated above, I confess that, while under other circumstances their dissatisfaction would not have influenced my action at all, it had the effect of simply confirming my decision already reached, to tender my resignation. This I did immediately on the assembling of the Board at their office, after breakfast."

In May of 1874, the Board of Trustees of the newly formed Southwestern Presbyterian University accepted the proposal of the city of Clarksville, Tennessee, to be the home of their institution. One year later, in May of 1875, the man was born who fifty years later would remove that college from Clarksville—and give the College not just a new campus, but a new name and new life.

Charles Edward Diehl was born in Charles Town (as it was then known), West Virginia. His father was a marble and granite dealer, so it was perhaps in the family business that Diehl developed his lifelong appreciation of stonework.

In Diehl's own words, "I was an only child, sickly and afflicted with heart trouble, which restricted my boyhood activities, especially in the matter of normal sports. Consequently, I was prepared for college by tutors."

In 1896 he received his A.B. from Johns Hopkins University, an outstanding liberal arts college whose motto—"*Veritas vos liberabit*"—would forever be a part of Diehl's values. He continued his education at Princeton University, where in 1900 he received his M.A. degree, graduated from the Princeton Theological Seminary, and was ordained as a minister.

His pastoral career began with the churches of Crescent Springs and Independence, Kentucky, from 1900 to 1905. He then served two years in Greenville, Mississippi, where he met the woman who in 1909 would become his wife, Katherine Ireys.

After only two years in Greenville, Diehl was called to the pulpit of First Church in Clarksville, Tennessee. Energetic and outgoing, Diehl quickly became a popular and important figure in the Clarksville community. He was one of the founders of the local Rotary Club and was also active in organizing the Boy Scouts and the United Charities. In 1909 he accepted a one-term replacement position teaching Biblical Languages and Literature at Southwestern Presbyterian

Charles Edward Diehl: President, 1917-49
"Genuineness and excellence"

University and the following year the University honored him with a Doctor of Divinity degree.

So he was no stranger to the institution when it called upon him to assume the presidency in 1917. The previous President, J.R. Dobyns, had resigned in the middle of the 1916-17 year, feeling that he lacked support from the Board for his "forward movement" to increase the enrollment and endowment of the College. George Lang, Professor of History and Vice-President, served as Acting President until the end of the school year in June, when the position was offered to Diehl.

It was a difficult choice for Diehl. He was at that time seriously considering the offer of the pastorate of a Chicago church "at a very substantial salary." Already weakened by poor morale and ongoing financial problems, the University had just lost half of its 119 students due to the entry of the United States into World War I in April 1917. Accepting the presidency "seemed to be a precarious undertaking," but after long and careful thought, he did so "out of a sense of duty and as a venture of faith."

Faith was certainly necessary in the next two years as he shepherded the school through its wartime exigencies, brought women students into the College on an equal basis with men, and struggled within his own mind as to whether the College could be sustained in Clarksville. In 1919 he agreed with those who wanted to move the school to Memphis, and set in motion a project that would consume him for the next six years.

During those six years he juggled numerous tasks: he directed the affairs of the College and taught in its Bible course; worked with the fundraising committee on a daily basis to secure the $1.5 million needed for the move; selected the actual site (and negotiated a considerable reduction in the cost of the property); toured the country interviewing architects; worked with the selected architect to design the new campus; supervised every detail of the building of that campus ("I do not believe that the kitchen as now planned is adequate or effective"); and bought a stone quarry in Arkansas.

Nor did his labors cease with the opening of the new campus on September 24, 1925. With the campus still far from complete and the mortgage to be retired, Diehl's goals for the

Dr. Diehl's Famous "Oil Can"

In 1955, Dr. Diehl explained the legendary "oil can" fund which he had used to assist members of the faculty and staff who were "confronted with emergencies and financial problems which were difficult to handle in view of the low salary scale of the College":

"I opened a bank account in the name of Charles E. Diehl, Special, in which I placed from time to time small amounts out of my own limited funds. I thought of this small fund as my 'oil can.' Several of my friends and a few alumni of the College voluntarily gave me sums of various amounts to be placed in the 'oil can' account and to be used as occasion required. The fund was never large.

"Out of this fund it has been possible to assist, either with a small gift or a loan, many members of the faculty and staff who were in unusual need because of illness, death in the family, or other emergencies. A few faculty members have been aided in a small way in their graduate work. Also, especially during the depression years, a number of students were enabled to remain in college through assistance from this fund."

Katherine Ireys Diehl:
"A just appreciation"

In Clarksville, President and Mrs. Diehl and their son Charles enjoyed the comforts of the two-story home on the campus built by Chancellor Summey in the 1890s. But when the College was moved to its much larger quarters in Memphis, the Diehls were not so fortunate. Although the original plans for the campus included an attractive two-story President's House at the base of the proposed tower at the west end of Palmer Hall, there was not enough money to build the tower or the house in 1925. So they moved into an apartment that had been created for them at the south end of Neely Hall.

In these early Memphis years, Mrs. Diehl was a familiar and reassuring presence to the students as she sat beneath the trees outside Neely, sewing and visiting with the students. In the *Southwestern Alumni Magazine* of May/June 1933, the following "Just Appreciation of Mrs. Diehl" appeared:

"Mrs. Diehl has made Southwestern mean much to Memphis. Grateful alumni and friends thank Dr. Diehl for the beauty and suitability of the college buildings, but it is Mrs. Diehl who has supervised the planting and the care of the beds of iris bordering the drives, the roses climbing over the fences, and the clumps of jonquils scattered about in the grove of trees.

"All Southwestern students are Mrs. Diehl's own. Her generous friendship finds them even before they know they need her and it endures undiminished after their graduation. Perhaps it is because she establishes a warm informality by the use of each student's given name; surely it is because of her 'little, nameless, unremembered acts of kindness and love' that she creates around her, in contrast to the academic atmosphere of Palmer Hall, the fragrant atmosphere of the home."

The entrance to the Diehls' apartment in Neely Hall bore witness to Mrs. Diehl's love of flowers.

College were set even higher.

Five years later, in October of 1930, as the College struggled with the effects of the Depression, Diehl endured a personal ordeal: a group of local ministers charged him with heresy and financial recklessness in the management of the College. A hearing before the Board of Directors unanimously cleared him of all charges.

In 1941, Diehl's success as a Christian educator was reflected in the two significant positions he occupied that year—Moderator of the General Assembly of the Church and President of the American Association of Colleges.

Diehl announced his decision to retire in 1944, as he neared the mandatory retirement age of seventy, but the Board requested that he stay until 1947 to see the $2.5 million Pre-Centennial Endowment Fund campaign to its conclusion. The success of this campaign in Memphis and throughout the Synods was a fitting final tribute to the man who had given so much of himself to the College. His official departure from the presidency was observed during the ceremonies marking the College's centennial year in 1949.

Of course, Diehl never really departed from the College. His advice was frequently sought and generously given. As his eyesight failed in later years, a succession of students, faculty, and alumni gladly became his readers. For his eightieth birthday he was serenaded by the entire student body. He died on February 27, 1964, in his eighty-ninth year.

When Diehl became President of the College in 1917 it had plant and endowment assets of $400,000; when he retired thirty-two years later, those assets were in excess of $5 million. But the greatest endowment he left the College were the ideals that guided his life and were expressed in the words engraved beneath his statue: *genuineness and excellence.*

Peyton Nalle Rhodes: President, 1949-65

"Zeal for knowledge has been his polestar and the pursuit of excellence his course"

—Inscription on plaque in Frazier Jelke Science Center honoring Dr. Rhodes

PNR. From 1949 to 1965 these initials were "the official stamp, the unequivocal authority, the ultimate word in the college community," according to the anonymous author of a retirement tribute to Peyton Nalle Rhodes in 1965. More than that, though, to his friends and faculty the initials were an affectionate nickname, a way to reduce the impressive syllables of his name to an accessible, unpretentious handle that corresponded to the man's own qualities.

He was given that splendid name by his proud parents in Crozet, Virginia, on the day of his birth, January 29, 1900. After grammar school and high school in Clifton Forge, Virginia, he entered the University of Virginia, where he was a member of the Raven Society and Phi Beta Kappa. He received his B.A. in chemistry in 1920, his M.A. one year later, and his Ph.D. in physics in 1926. He spent the years 1922 to 1924 teaching chemistry and physics at Woodberry Forest School in Orange, Virginia, subjects he was to later teach (as well as Spanish) at the University while he was working on his doctorate.

Soon after earning his Ph.D., Rhodes was recruited by Dr. Diehl to move to the new Southwestern campus in Memphis as Assistant Professor of Physics. He returned briefly to Virginia in 1927 to claim his college sweetheart, Alice Boisseau Archer, as his bride. In 1929, he was elevated to

full professorship.

During World War II, Rhodes served as coordinator of the Thirteenth College Training Detachment (Aircrew) on the campus and was named Vice-President of the College in 1944.

When Diehl retired in 1949, the Board of Trustees unanimously chose Rhodes to succeed him, with Diehl's wholehearted support: "I am delighted to turn over the presidency to him, feeling assured that the standards and high quality of work at Southwestern will be continued. I have the greatest confidence in Dr. Rhodes' rock-ribbed integrity."

Diehl's confidence was well-placed. A brief summary of Rhodes' accomplishments in the sixteen years of his presidency can only suggest his lasting and enormous contributions: ten major

Peyton Rhodes
Didn't Lose His Dignity

The Hula Hoop Experience

It was 1958 and the world was mad for the hula hoop. So mad that the normally staid Rotary Club of Memphis included a hula hoop competition as part of the fun at its annual picnic.

And the winner was ... Dr. Peyton Nalle Rhodes, President of Southwestern at Memphis!

When this hip-shaking event was reported the following day by *Memphis Press-Scimitar* writer Mary Allie Taylor '33, her account included PNR's insightful (and typically witty) explanation of his success:

"Actually, what is involved is the conservation of angular momentum, something that should certainly be conserved by all and sundry. It is merely necessary to exert a small, but carefully regulated impulse (the product of force × time) by allowing a hypersensitive sacroiliac to impinge on a small portion of the interior periphery of a short section of the hoop. The impulse, applied with some discretion, serves to produce a change in the angular momentum of the hoop, and if the force of this impulse is so directed that there is a small vertical component of this momentum opposing the force of gravity which acts uniformly over the plane of the hoop, then the resulting horizontal motion will be maintained with rare uniformity to the amazement of all beholders who do not realize that the whole deal is just as easy as falling off a log."

A hula-hooping college president was too good a story for the wire services to pass up, and soon Rhodes was receiving congratulations from colleagues and delighted alumni across the country. There was even an editorial in the *New York Post*.

But it was the editorial page of the *Press-Scimitar* that expressed the universal view of the community most succinctly. Under the headline PEYTON RHODES DIDN'T LOSE HIS DIGNITY, the editors observed:

"Someone remarked when he read the news that President Peyton Rhodes of Southwestern had won the hula hoop championship at the Rotary picnic and saw the picture of him in the act in Saturday's *Press-Scimitar*: 'Peyton Rhodes is one of the few college presidents I know who could do that and not lose his dignity.'

THE TERRE HAUTE STAR, FRIDAY, OCTOBER 3, 1958.

STRICTLY SCIENTIFIC—The current hula hooping craze has reached even the hallowed halls of ivy, where it is now recognized as just a matter of Newton's laws of motion. At Southwestern College in Memphis, Tenn., President Peyton N. Rhodes utilizes the physics he formerly taught to whirl the hoop as an unbelieving coed pauses in the background.

"Peyton Rhodes has the sureness of himself and the rightness of his purpose that gives him such a sense of security that he needs no shell of false dignity to protect him. Hence his naturalness and outspokenness. He looks all right in a cap and gown and also in a hula hoop."

buildings, including Burrow Library, Mallory Gymnasium and the Halliburton Tower, were added to the College's existing eight; enrollment increased from 600 to 900; a campus chapter of Phi Beta Kappa was founded; financial support from the church and national foundations was increased; and total assets grew from $5 million to nearly $14 million.

Rhodes was in every sense a hands-on president, whether he was pulling an errant weed from a campus flower bed, checking for dust in a campus phone booth, or supervising every construction detail in a new building. After his retirement in 1965, he served as consultant for construction of the Frazier Jelke Science Center complex. He also returned to the presidential desk in Halliburton Tower for a four-month period in late 1969 while the trustees sought a replacement for Dr. David Alexander. In 1979 he returned once more as Acting Vice-President and Dean. In 1981, the College honored him by naming the six-story physics building the Peyton Nalle Rhodes Tower.

Three years later, when the Board of Trustees had decided that the confusing Southwestern name needed to be retired, the solution seemed obvious: name it after the man who had served the College so well for more than fifty years of his life.

Accordingly, on July 1, 1984, the College recognized Peyton Nalle Rhodes for the incalculable gifts he had bestowed upon it in his more than fifty years of service: his devotion, warmth, scholarship, wit, vision, and inspiring example. Said Board Chairman Frank M. Mitchener, Jr. when the name change was announced, "We do not honor a benefactor in the traditional sense; rather, we honor one who has given his life to Southwestern."

A Consort of Grace and Charm

She was born Alice Boisseau Archer in Hermitage, Virginia—a town she once described as "two gas stations and a telephone pole"—where her father was a country doctor. She attended Hollins and Mary Baldwin College before marrying Peyton Rhodes, the young physics professor who whisked her away to Memphis in 1927.

Her natural friendliness made her an invaluable asset to campus life. Of her early days on the small Southwestern campus she said, "I knew the first names of all the people there—I knew every student." And they all knew Mrs. Rhodes—and loved her. In appreciation for years of faithful attendance at football games, hosting official functions, welcoming visitors, raising money for scholarships, and giving of herself unselfishly to the whole college community, she was honored in 1972 by the Southwestern Women's Club with the creation of the Alice Archer Rhodes Scholarship Fund.

Dr. and Mrs. Rhodes hosted a party honoring Lisa Rollow, daughter of Mr. and Mrs. John Rollow.

James Harold Daughdrill, Jr.:

President, 1973-

"Inspires with his energy, challenges with his intellect . . . warms with his faith."

—Ralph Jones III, alumnus and trustee

This college was built by brave men. Included in that number must certainly be those intrepid members of the Board of Trustees who, in January 1973, broke with the tradition of choosing educators to run a college and chose as their eighteenth president a man with no experience in managing an institution of higher learning, a man who had spent half his career as a businessman.

But this seemingly unlikely prospect had been the unanimous choice of two selection committees, one comprised of ten board members (five were alumni), the other an advisory committee of five faculty members and three students. At the press conference announcing their choice, Acting Board President Van Pritchartt said, "With Jim Daughdrill coming to take over the presidency, we look forward to the best days ever."

The twenty-five years (to date) of the Daughdrill presidency bear witness to the wisdom of the committees and the perspicacity of Mr. Pritchartt. By all measurable standards, as it celebrates its 150th anniversary in 1998, the College *is* enjoying its "best days ever."

James H. Daughdrill, Jr. started his life in that part of the country that could almost be called the cradle of the College's presidents, the southeastern United States. He was born in LaGrange, Georgia, on April 25, 1934, and graduated in 1952 from Chattanooga's McCallie School (founded by a graduate of the same college that Daughdrill would someday head).

After two years at Davidson College, where he was president of his sophomore class, Daughdrill married his high school sweetheart, Elizabeth Anne Gay, and transferred to Emory University in Atlanta. In 1956 he received his B.A. in English from Emory and entered his father's textile business in Cartersville, Georgia.

By 1958 the younger Daughdrill was president of the carpet division of the company, and the following year he was elected to membership in the Young President's Organization International. In 1961 he was named Cartersville's "Young Man of the Year" and elected to the Board of Directors of the National Carpet Institute. He was a young man on the fast track to success.

But in 1964, at the age of thirty, according to his wife, "We were happy, but something was missing." Daughdrill explained it this way: "There are human dimensions that business just didn't have, and I wasn't fulfilled as a whole human being." Daughdrill had seriously considered the ministry while he was in college and now the call to the church had returned, even stronger than before.

So they sold their home and moved to Decatur, Georgia, where Daughdrill enrolled in Columbia Theological Seminary and Libby Daughdrill took a job as a secretary at the First Baptist Church. At Columbia, Daughdrill served a year as president of the student body before receiving his Master of Divinity degree *magna cum laude* in 1967. Later that year the young family (there were now two Daughdrill children, with a third soon to appear) moved to Little Rock and its first pastorate, St. Andrew's Presbyterian Church. Within a year, Daughdrill was president of the Little Rock Presbyterian Ministers Association. The presidential title just seemed to come naturally wherever he went.

Wider horizons in the church beckoned, and in 1970 Daughdrill accepted the position of Secretary of Stewardship for the Presbyterian Church in the United States. It was here, in 1973, that he came to the attention of the Southwestern search committees.

Southwestern was seeking "a man of highest personal integrity ... a proven leader, an experienced administrator, someone who could represent Southwestern well before all its publics." In Daughdrill, the school found all of that—and much more.

The school found a man who could stop the rising tide of debt that threatened the stability and growth of the College. He soon erased the red ink that had characterized the previous six years, and the school has operated in the black ever since.

The school found a man who could define the mission of the College, who could clearly state its governing values and its Christian commitment. A man who could put modern organizational skills at the service of that noblest of professions, the training of young minds. A man who could raise faculty salaries until they ranked in the top twenty percent of small

Daughdrill Takes the Chair

One look at his list of accomplishments makes it clear that Jim Daughdrill was born to lead. In addition to the various presidencies that have marked his career, he has found time to serve as chairman of a number of professional organizations. Here are some of the major committees, councils, and boards he has headed at various times in the past twenty-four years:

- **Association of American Colleges and Universities**

- **National Advisory Committee on Accreditation, U.S. Department of Education**

- **Southern College and University Union**

- **Southern University Conference**

- **Tennessee Council of Private Colleges**

- **Southern College Athletic Conference**

- **Memphis Chapter, National Conference of Christians and Jews**

- **Association of Presbyterian Colleges**

Several times a year, Daughdrill sits at a table in the Refectory at lunchtime with his AT&T sign, inviting students to Ask the President, Tell the President, Talk to the President.

A Few Things You May Not Know About Jim Daughdrill

- **Collects model Volkswagen Beetles**
- **Cuts his own hair**
- **Serves his wife coffee in bed every morning**
- **Meditates an hour each morning, and spends a week of silent retreat in a Trappist monastery every year**
- **Eats Snickers candy bars**
- **Some of his heroes: Beethoven, Robert Frost, Emily Dickinson, Karl Barth, Thomas Merton, Charles E. Diehl**
- **Has six grandchildren and two cats**
- **Likes to end his day with an Auturo Fuente Double Chateau cigar**

liberal arts colleges, and could see the average SAT scores of incoming students rise from 1105 to 1288.

In an unprecedented action in 1979, the trustees awarded Daughdrill a ten-year contract. This action was taken, in the words of Dr. Paul Tudor Jones, trustee and alumnus, "to express its confidence in his leadership and to safeguard the future of the College." In 1989, that contract was renewed for a second ten-year term.

Daughdrill's achievements have not been attained without stresses. There have

been disagreements over tenure, faculty evaluation methods, and intellectual diversity. But most have been the kind that arise any time a group of bright people with strong opinions get together. And the discourse has been reasoned, the arguments have been civil—most of the time.

The physical expansion of the College has continued under Daughdrill, with eight new buildings added, including the most recent, the Bryan Campus Life Center, the largest facility on the campus. Major renovations to existing buildings have preserved the College's valuable architectural heritage while preparing it for further years of service.

The financial growth during the Daughdrill years has been little short of phenomenal: the endowment has increased to $207 million and total assets of the College have increased by $300 million.

With this healthy fiscal picture, enrollment at an all-time high (1,463), and national media recognition for the quality of the school, Rhodes College is stronger, better equipped, and more fully prepared to carry out its mission than at any time in its long history. Jim Daughdrill's manifold accomplishments guarantee him an honored place in that history.

The Daughdrill Family

(standing, left of stairs)
David Hoover and daughter Katie

(sitting on step)
Gay Daughdrill Boyd and son Battle Boyd

(standing behind Gay on left with child)
Hal Boyd III and son Hal Boyd IV

(standing behind Gay on right)
John Hoover and his mother Risha Daughdrill Hoover

(second row from top, left to right)
Elizabeth Gay Daughdrill, Jim Daughdrill, his mother Vickie Daughdrill, and his sister Meg Daughdrill

(top row, left to right)
James H. Daughdrill, Hal Daughdrill

Elizabeth Gay Daughdrill: A Full-Time Partner

In political circles, Libby Daughdrill would be known as an "activist" wife; she takes her responsibilities as the College's first lady as seriously as her husband takes his presidential duties. As former Board Chairman Robert McCallum put it, "When they're on the road, it's like two people working for the College instead of one."

And the Daughdrills are on the road a lot—meeting alumni, introducing Rhodes to prospective students and their parents, helping to raise money for the endowment, sharing their enthusiasm for the College with everyone they meet.

The Daughdrill team is far more than a "road show," of course. When they're at home, they have a full calendar of college events: dinners and receptions to host, lectures to attend, sporting activities to cheer, visiting dignitaries to entertain.

Libby Daughdrill seems to have been born to fill the role. Her warm smile and Southern manners (she grew up in Atlanta) can put anyone at ease—from a nervous freshman to an international economics lecturer.

Making people feel welcome is certainly an essential part of a first lady's assignment, but Libby is much more to Rhodes than a gracious hostess. In addition to supervising all official entertaining, she has worked in the office of the Dean of Students, served on planning committees for college events, and handled social correspondence for the presidential office.

But her most lasting contribution has been in interior design. Libby has accepted the responsibility for seeing that the College's social rooms maintain the Rhodes style and quality in their furnishings. Just as her husband has preserved the architectural integrity of the campus buildings, she has seen that the interiors reflect the same dignity and warmth.

As great as her devotion to Rhodes has been and as much of herself as she has given to it, the College must still take second place in her affections. For Jim and Libby Daughdrill, their family has always been and will ever be first in their hearts. The Daughdrills' three children—Hal, Risha and Gay—are grown now with children of their own, but the entire family still gets together at Easter and Thanksgiving and arranges an annual vacation at a place that offers recreation for toddlers, teenagers, parents, and grandparents alike.

In 1997, Libby honored her own parents and the College by establishing the annual Walter E. Gay Award for the outstanding male athlete of the year and the Rebecca Rish Gay Award for the outstanding female athlete. She noted at the time that this award was prompted by her parents' indomitable spirit and their love for young people. That their daughter has inherited these admirable qualities is evident to everyone who meets Libby Daughdrill.

Libby Daughdrill with tennis coach Sarah Hatgas and Rebecca Rish Gay award-winner Nao Kinoshita.

"A college may be better than its material advantages. It is never better than its faculty."

—Charles E. Diehl, Southwestern Bulletin, June 1932

To anyone who loves learning, there is something profoundly moving about an academic procession. To witness the parade of scholars in their medieval gowns, their colorful and symbolic hoods and headgear, is to make a personal connection with one of humankind's noblest traditions. For collectively, the men and women in these processions carry within their minds the wisdom, the discoveries, and the experience of our entire culture, and every day they pass on that priceless inheritance to a new generation.

Great teachers have always been and will ever be the principal strength of this institution, the foundation upon which it rests. At the opening convocation of the College's session in 1950, President Emeritus Charles E. Diehl reiterated from his famous 1925 "Ideals of Southwestern" speech the school's unchanging position on the role of the faculty: "The teacher is always the most important part of the college. He is the college in the active sense; all other things are circumstance, machinery, arrangements. He is the mind that learns and teaches, the character and personality that influences, and becomes a never to be forgotten memory for good or ill."

The first meeting of the faculty in 1849, though historic, was not eventful.

Proceedings
of the
Faculty
of the
Masonic University of Tennessee

1st Meeting
Feb. 19th 1849

The first meeting of the Faculty was held at the house of Professor A. B. Russell, on Monday, February 19th 1849.

Present, all the members, viz;

All present.

W. F. Hopkins, Pres.t & Prof. Math. & Nat. Sci—

I. Guillet, Prof. Anc.t & Mod. Languages

Rev. A. B. Russell, Adj.ct Prof. Anc.t Lan; and
Prin. Prep. Depart.t

Statutes &
Reg. approv.

The President submitted the regulations and Statutes, drafted by himself, for the government of this institution. Having been read, Considered and approved, they were ordered to be presented to the Board of Trustees, for their sanction.

No further business appearing, the Faculty

Adjourned

adjourned.

W. F. Hopkins

[No Sec.y of the Faculty yet appointed]

President

Meetings of the Faculty were neglected, untill Saturday, May 26th, when the members were convened by a summons from the President.

2.d Meeting
May 26. 1849

Saturday May 26th 1849. The Faculty met, at the Trustees' room, in the Masonic Hall, at 9 o'clk A.M.

Present all the members, viz;

W. F. Hopkins, Pres.t & Prof. Math. & Nat. Sci—

All present

Isidore Guillet, Prof. Anc.t & Modern Languages

& also

Rev. A. B. Russell, Prin. Prep. Dept. & Adg.t Prof. L—

The Faculty Maintains Discipline

In the days before deans, the disciplining of students was a responsibility of the faculty. The minutes of the college faculty meetings chronicle an interesting array of student infractions.

On March 31, 1851, the minutes note that four students "were examined as to the parts they severally took in a mock duel on Saturday, March 29." All were suspended, and a young instructor in the preparatory department was dismissed for his participation in the affair.

The following month, two students were brought before the faculty for "using profane language, quarreling and menacing (Mr. Guerin using a stick) and by Mr. Guerin making a personal assault upon Mr. Dixon. When before the faculty, Mr. Dixon exhibited penitence and humility, but Mr. Guerin gave no token of regret." For his intransigence, Mr. Guerin was expelled.

But the faculty could be forgiving as well. On March 23, 1880, "The Chancellor having had an interview with Mr. Pepper, in view of his candid confession of his weakness and his great abhorrence of it, coupled with his great desire to escape, if possible, from his craving for drink, and also in view of his great desire to remain in the institution on honorable terms, it was resolved that we give him another trial in all kindness believing that he will reciprocate it in an honorable way and hoping that he may be more successful in the future."

The fear of bad public relations made things worse for two students charged with "disgraceful conduct" in May 7, 1883, when the faculty, "considering that there could be no doubt of the guilt of the parties, recognizing that the circumstances being known to the citizens of the town, the matter would occasion scandal in the community detrimental to the character of the University, decided that the above-named students be summarily dismissed."

At times the faculty felt called upon to issue warnings. On February 7, 1896, "it was moved and carried that the students be informed that card-playing is contrary to the rules of the Institution, and that anyone who is known to be guilty of it will be held subject to discipline."

And on September 29, 1915, in a foreshadowing of today's Social Regulations Council, the faculty recommended "that the functions of the Honor Council be extended to the general oversight of the moral conduct of the student body, that the Honor Council be empowered to take cognizance of such things as: intemperance, gambling, licentiousness, cheating in recitations, in fact all conduct unbecoming to a gentleman and a student of the University."

"A surprising and most gratifying fact"

When John N. Waddel took the leadership of Southwestern Presbyterian University in 1879, he had already served as the head of two colleges, LaGrange College in Tennessee and the University of Mississippi in Oxford. He was much impressed with the quality of the faculty he found in Clarksville. In his autobiography he states:

"It has always been to me a surprising, and yet a most gratifying fact, that the Southwestern Presbyterian University has been so highly favored as to retain in service for so long a period Professors of such acknowledged ability as those occupying the several chairs of instruction in the Faculty. It is not, by any means, an extravagant estimate of the merit justly accorded to these gentlemen, that they would have been found, respectively, fully equal to any similar position in any of the institutions of the higher learning in the country."

The Faculty of 1895

The ten professors who sat for this portrait in 1895 were among the best-loved and most-honored SPU faculty members of the last half of the nineteenth century. In their scholarship, wide-ranging interests, and devotion to their students, these men represent the kind of teaching that characterized the school in the nineteenth century.

1 Rev. George Summey, D.D.
Chancellor

Summey, Chancellor of the University from 1892-1902, came to SPU from a pastorate in Chester, South Carolina. A graduate of Davidson College, he had also studied at Union Theological Seminary. His term as Chancellor was marked by the addition of the Waddel Building and Calvin Hall. It was Summey who pressed the school's Civil War damage claim against the U.S. government, resulting in the award of $25,000 to the school. In the SPU yearbook of 1899, the students paid him this tribute: "Dr. Summey possesses the two qualities now expected in the head of a literary institution, culture and scholarship combined with executive ability and a talent for business."

2 Edward B. Massie
Professor of Mathematics

A student at the University of Virginia when the Civil War began, Massie joined the Army of Northern Virginia and was wounded three times. He belonged to a family of distinguished teachers: one brother taught at Washington and Lee, one at the University of Virginia, and one became Chancellor of the University of Tennessee. Massie's mathematics courses were among the most popular on campus. The SPU *Journal* said of him: "No man has ever been connected with the faculty of the SPU whose influence with the students has been greater or more wholesome than that of Mr. Massie. This is due both to his pre-eminent ability and untiring patience as an instructor, and to his justice and kindness in all his dealings with his pupils."

3 Thomas Oakley Deaderick
Professor of Latin and French

A native of east Tennessee, Deaderick received his education at the University of Tennessee and taught at his alma mater and West Florida Seminary before joining the Southwestern faculty. His father served for many years as Clerk of the Supreme Court of Tennessee, and his uncle served as Chief Justice of this state. The yearbook of 1899 notes that "Prof. Deaderick is skillful in imparting instruction and in stimulating his students to a high degree of excellence. He is a cultivated musician, is gifted with a very fine voice, and often contributes by his talents in this line to the pleasure of social gatherings in Clarksville and University circles."

4 Robert Alexander Webb
Professor of Systematic Theology

The son of a Mississippi planter who moved north to Nashville after the Civil War, Webb attended the famous Webb School (no relation) and entered Stewart College in 1874. He graduated in 1877 as valedictorian of his class and then entered Columbia Theological Seminary. He returned to his alma mater in 1892 to teach in the Theology School. The SPU *Journal* noted of him: "As a preacher he is earnest and eloquent, and proclaims the Word with power and simplicity. As a theologian, he is recognized as one of the ablest, soundest and most conservative in our church. As a teacher it is not too much to say, for it is the universal verdict of his classes, that he 'was born' for the place and is unexcelled."

the most enduring. He continued teaching until he was eighty-two. Born in Mississippi, he received his theological training at the Princeton Seminary and returned to his native state, where he served several pastorates before joining the Southwestern faculty in 1882. During his long teaching career, Price occupied chairs in history, English, and ecclesiastical history. The 1899 yearbook said of him: "Dr. Price is noted for his sound and clear views on questions of state and church. He also has a ready wit, which enlivens his conversation. As a preacher he is forcible and impressive; as a teacher he imparts to his students an interest in their work."

7 Rev. William A. Alexander
Professor of Biblical Languages and Literature

A graduate of the University of Mississippi in the Class of 1875, Alexander received prizes in Latin, mathematics, and Shakespeare. Immediately after graduation he was appointed a tutor in physics and astronomy while he earned his M.A. He attended Princeton Seminary and came to SPU in 1892. The yearbook comments: "Dr. Alexander is a man of scholarly attainments, which he is constantly increasing by close study. He gives his students a thorough training in the important branches which are committed to his charge."

5 George Frederick Nicolassen
Professor of Greek and German

Nicolassen's educational itinerary includes two institutions very familiar to this school: the University of Virginia (B.A., M.A.) and Johns Hopkins University (Ph.D.). An accomplished musician, he conducted the musical part of the school's daily chapel exercises. Nicolassen also founded and served as drillmaster of the "University Grays," a drill team that provided physical training for the students in the pregymnasium days. The yearbook of 1899 observed: "Dr. Nicolassen is a man of few words, but those the right words, characterized by vigor, clearness and directness. His classes are large and there is no light or slighted work in them. They are noted for the frequency of the annual 'encores' for which he calls. He will not pass a man on to a higher class until the man is ready for it."

6 Rev. Robert Price
Professor of History

At sixty-five, Rev. Price was the oldest member of the faculty when this photograph was taken—and destined to be

8 James Adair Lyon
Professor of Natural Sciences

Three generations of Lyon's family played large roles in the history of this college. His father was one of the leaders of the movement to create a Presbyterian university in the 1870s and served on SPU's first Board of Directors. Lyon himself joined the faculty in 1885, after receiving his Ph.D. from Princeton. His son Scott graduated from SPU and studied at the University of Virginia before returning to teach with his father. Lyon was very popular with the student body, partly because of his support and encouragement of the school's athletic activities.

The two unidentified men in the photo are probably **Thornton Whaling**, who taught philosophy and practical theology from 1892 to 1896, and **Eugene R. Long**, who taught English from 1895 to 1897.

Where Did You Get Your Degree?

The academic credentials of the College's earliest faculty members are not available to us today. Although the 1855 catalogue of Stewart College boasts that "two of its seven faculty members hold A.M. degrees, one has an M.D., and one a D.D.," we have no record of where those degrees were earned.

But when the faculty for the session of 1870-71 (the first under President Shearer) was announced, the Clarksville *Tobacco Leaf* proudly announced that four of the five professors were graduates of the University of Virginia, and two of the four "fairly won the degree of Master of Arts."

Virginia's voice on the faculty continued to be a strong one for the rest of the century. But the next discernible trend did not appear until the arrival of Dr. Charles E. Diehl. An M.A. from Princeton, Diehl had a strong preference for Ivy League graduates. Greatly impressed by the English universities' educational methods, Diehl also had a special fondness for Rhodes scholars, and several of that rare breed graced the College's faculty roster for a number of years.

A look at the advanced degrees of today's faculty does not reveal much of a trend in any special direction. Of the more than 140 full-time faculty on the 1997-98 roster, the largest number holding degrees from any one institution is ten—from Vanderbilt. The other schools represented on the Rhodes College faculty range all across the map and include some of the most prestigious names in American education, as well as several distinguished foreign universities.

The 1997-98 Rhodes College faculty represent over 50 American universities and three international ones.

A Haven for Fugitives

In the 1930s the College's cloistered walls literally became a haven for Fugitives when two members of that celebrated literary group taught here—the poets Robert Penn Warren and Allen Tate.

The Fugitives, as most English majors will recall, first convened at Vanderbilt in the 1920s, where several poets gathered

Robert Penn Warren, 1930   *Allen Tate, 1934*

to discuss their own poetry and that of others, and to publish it in their own magazine, *The Fugitive*. Besides Warren and Tate, the group included John Crowe Ransom, Donald Davidson, Merrill Moore, and John Gould Fletcher.

Warren came to the College in 1930 as a temporary replacement for Professor Samuel H. Monk, who was on leave of absence studying at Oxford. Monk had met Warren at Oxford and recommended him for the position. After a year in Memphis, Warren returned to Vanderbilt in a similar replacement spot.

The replacement position expired two years later, and Warren wrote Dr. Diehl about the possibility of a return to Memphis. Eager to have him back, Diehl offered a Lectureship in English, which Warren accepted. A few weeks later, however, Warren received a considerably better offer from Louisiana State University, where his friend Cleanth Brooks was teaching.

Warren then wrote Dr. Diehl in enthusiastic support of his long-time friend and fellow Fugitive Allen Tate for the position. Tate accepted the offer and spent the years 1934 to 1936 as Lecturer in English at Southwestern.

His classroom experience at Southwestern, Vanderbilt, and LSU persuaded Warren that there was no satisfactory textbook for the teaching of literary interpretation. Consequently, when he was working with Brooks at LSU, they collaborated on such a book, *Understanding Poetry*, which became a standard college text across the country for three decades after its publication.

Warren, widely honored as poet, novelist, and essayist, received two Pulitzer Prizes in poetry and one in fiction, and served as Poet Laureate at the Library of Congress. Tate was awarded the Bollingen Prize in poetry and was elected to the American Academy of Arts and Letters.

The Spirit
of the University

It is the cordial relation that exists between the Faculty and students.

Members of the Faculty do not hold themselves aloof, but are actually able to put themselves in the student's place and to see his problems with sympathy.

It helps a man to know that he has friends who are interested in him.

Every student here ought to be able to know that every member of the Faculty is his friend.

This page from the 1916 SPU Book of Facts defines one of the most valuable and enduring assets of the school, the close relationship between the faculty and the students.

Robert Penn Warren and Allen Tate were both awarded honorary degrees by the College—Warren in 1974 (shown right) and Tate in 1977.

A Gallery of Great Teachers

These wise faces light the walls of the Refectory, a constant reminder of the great teachers who have illuminated the life of this college. They were chosen for inclusion in the Distinguished Faculty Portrait Series by vote of the alumni in an ongoing process that adds a new portrait every year.

W. Raymond Cooper
1886-1959
Professor of History, Dean, friend and advisor to generations of students

John Quincy Wolf
1901-72
Professor of English, beloved and respected teacher, nationally known folklorist

Marion Leigh MacQueen
1896-1980
Professor of Mathematics, Department Chair, director of the College's move to Memphis

David Muir Amacker
1897-1985
Rhodes Scholar, interpreter at the drafting of the League of Nations, founder of Department of Political Science, Distinguished Professor 1936-69

Jack D. Farris
1921-
T.K. Young Professor of English 1961-84, novelist, playwright, poet, and mentor to generations of students

Fred William Neal
1915-97

Professor of Religion, 1958-85, Director of "Search for Values," inspiring and beloved teacher

Laurence F. Kinney
1902-66

A.B. Curry Professor of Bible and Religion, 1943-66, co-founder of "Search for Values," an intellectual and spiritual leader

John Henry Davis
1899-1975

Rhodes Scholar, Professor of History 1926-69, a founder of the College's tutorial system, celebrated for his brilliance and wit

Charles Ireys Diehl
1910-96

Dean of Men, Professor of Education and English 1947-76, taught with wisdom, compassion, and wry-humored style

Robert Lewis Amy
1919-

Professor and Chair of the Department of Biology 1958-86, distinguished teacher and research pioneer

Danforth R. Ross
1911-98

Professor of English 1955-74, imparted his love of literature to students with wit, wisdom, and warmth

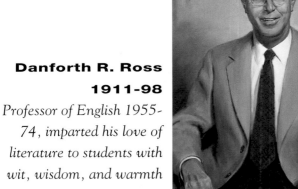

Alexander P. Kelso
1887-1963

Professor of Philosophy and Christian Ethics, 1925-57, R.A. Webb Chair, helped found tutorial and honors courses and "Search for Values"

In addition to the Distinguished Faculty Portrait series, the College Gallery includes portraits of revered faculty commissioned by friends, alumni, and colleagues to express their respect and affection for the teachers so honored.

Charles Louis Townsend
1887-1962
Professor of English, 1917-54, proud cap-wearer, cherished campus personality

Margaret Huxtable Townsend
1882-1970
Professor of Sociology, 1918-54, the College's first woman professor, first Dean of Women

A. Theodore Johnson
1890-1979
Professor of English, 1926-61, Dean of the College 1934-55, scholar and master of the bon mot

James Edgar Roper
1918-90
Professor of English, 1954-89, author of Southwestern at Memphis 1948-1975, noted historian and master of the limerick

Granville Daniel Davis
1909-76
Professor of History, 1954-76, Dean of Continuing Education, founder of Institute for Executive Leadership

Ralph Clifford Hon
1903-
Professor of Economics, 1931-73, mentor and benefactor to countless students

Yerger Hunt Clifton
1930-93
Professor of English, 1965-93, creator and longtime Dean of British Studies at Oxford

Honoring the Faculty

The College has always taken great pride in the achievements of its faculty. Thanks to the generosity of Rhodes benefactor Clarence Day of Memphis, this pride has taken a more demonstrative form with the awarding of significant cash prizes recognizing outstanding teaching and research and creative activity. The Charles E. Diehl Society also awards a generous prize each year in recognition of faculty service to the college community-at-large.

Clarence Day Award for Outstanding Teaching

1981	**Dr. Jack U. Russell**, Mathematics
1982	**Dr. Marshall E. McMahon**, Economics
1983	**Dr. William Larry Lacy**, Philosophy
1984	**Dr. James M. Vest**, French
1985	**Dr. Fred W. Neal**, Religious Studies
1986	**Dr. E. Llewellyn Queener**, Psychology
1987	**Dr. Rebecca Sue Legge**, Business Administration
1988	**Dr. Terry W. Hill**, Biology
1989	**Dr. F. Michael McLain**, Religious Studies
1990	**Dr. Cynthia Marshall**, English
1991	**Dr. William T. Jolly**, Classics
1992	**Dr. G. Kenneth Williams**, Mathematics
1993	**Dr. Jennifer Brady**, English
1994	**Dr. Horst R. Dinkelacker**, Foreign Languages and Literature
1995	**Dr. Carolyn R. Jaslow**, Biology
1996	**Prof. Julia Ewing**, Theatre
1997	**Dr. Bradford D. Penley**, Chemistry

Dean's Award for Research and Creative Activity

1981	**Dr. John F. Copper**, International Studies
1983	**Prof. Jack D. Farris**, English
1984	**Dr. Richard D. Gilliom**, Chemistry
1985	**Dr. David H. Kesler**, Biology
1986	**Prof. Tony Lee Garner**, Theatre
1987	**Dr. James M. Olcese**, Biology
1988	**Dr. John F. Copper**, International Studies
1989	**Dr. Alan P. Jaslow**, Biology
1990	**Dr. Jack H. Taylor**, Physics
1991	**Dr. Marcus D. Pohlman**, Political Science
1992	**Dr. Steven L. McKenzie**, Religious Studies
1993	**Dr. Robert J. Strandburg**, Psychology
1994	**Dr. Andrew A. Michta**, International Studies
1995	**Dr. Brian W. Shaffer**, English
1996	**Dr. Cynthia A. Marshall**, English
1997	**Dr. Stephen Haynes**, Religious Studies

Diehl Society Award for Service

1988	**Dr. Harold Lyons**, Chemistry
1989	**Dr. John S. Olsen**, Biology
1990	**Prof. David Ramsey**, Music
1991	**Dr. David Y. Jeter**, Chemistry
1992	**Dr. Gail C. McClay**, Education
1993	**Dr. Robert L. Llewellyn**, Philosophy
1994	**Dr. Douglas W. Hatfield**, History
1995	**Dr. Rebecca Sue Legge**, Business Administration
1996	**Dr. Charles C. Orvis**, Economics
1997	**Dr. Donald Tucker**, Spanish

1996 Day Award winner Julia Ewing with Clarence Day.

1997 Dean's Award winner Stephen Haynes with Clarence Day.

1995 Diehl Award winner Rebecca Sue Legge with Diehl Society President James A. Thomas III '62.

"The best education for all of life is an education in the liberal arts and sciences."

—Rhodes College Catalogue, 1997–98

Chapter Four: The College Curriculum

A fundamental purpose of the College from the beginning has been a simple one: to teach its students to think; that is, to give them the background and methods of reasoning that are necessary to form an intelligent opinion and take appropriate action.

As the Rhodes Mission puts it: "The best way to prepare leaders of vision is to inspire them with the best that mankind has achieved—the best in the arts, the best in scientific experiments, the highest examples of society, the deepest understandings of religion. The study of the liberal arts and sciences does this best, for it holds before students what Whitehead called 'the habitual vision of greatness.'"

Although the curriculum has changed with the times and with the world, it has never varied from its original purpose. It continues to prepare men and women for a fuller life by giving them the means to analyze, evaluate, and judge.

A Brief History of the Curriculum

An unidentified chronicler in 1643 described the curriculum of Harvard College as "Latine and Greeke, and Disputations Logicall and Philosophicall." In 1855, just over two hundred years later, higher education had not changed very much, as witness the curriculum of Stewart College stated in its catalogue of that year.

The Stewart student was expected to devote his entire time to Greek, Latin, and mathematics throughout the first two years of study. In the third year, science courses replaced mathematics, and students were given their first option—a modern foreign language could replace Latin and Greek. In the last year, Latin and science courses continued, with the addition of philosophy, political science, and "Evidences of Christianity."

This arrangement remained essentially in place until 1872, when several slight changes appeared. Sophomores received "Introductory and Popular (Science) Courses," juniors were introduced to psychology, and seniors were required to take a "Review of Entire Course" in preparation for their comprehensive exams. Most important,

The 1872 curriculum introduced the four-year biblical course requirement.

8	CATALOGUE.

FRESHMAN CLASS.

FIRST TERM.

Virgil's Æneid.
Xenophon's Anabasis.
Latin Grammar, Andrews and Stoddard, reviewed.
Greek Grammar, Fisk's, reviewed.
Arnold's Latin and Greek Prose Composition, with written translations into English.
Algebra,   Bourdon.

SECOND TERM.

Livy,   Lincoln.
Exercises in Latin Composition.
Xenophon's Memorabilia,   Anthon.
Exercises in Greek Composition.
Geometry,   Legendre.

SOPHOMORE CLASS.

FIRST TERM.

Cicero de Senectute and de Amicitia.
Horace, Odes.
Exercises in Latin Composition.
Homer's Iliad.
Exercises in Greek Composition.
Roman and Grecian Antiquities.
Trigonometry and Surveying,   Davies.

SECOND TERM.

Horace, Satires.
Latin Composition.
Prometheus of Æschylus,   Woolsey.
Greek Composition.
Analytical Geometry,   Davies.

Every student at Stewart College in 1855 followed the same prescribed course of study.

CLASSIFICATION.

	Latin.	Greek.	Mathematics.	History.
FRESHMAN CLASS.	Horace and Livy, Prose Compos'n (Arnold,) Prosody.	Anabasis and Cyropædia. Prose Compos'n (Arnold.)	Higher Algebra and Geometry (Loomis.)	Ancient History and Geography.
	Latin.	**Greek.**	**Mathematics.**	**Sciences.**
SOPHOMORE CLASS,	Tacitus and Juvenal, Prose Composition, Prosody.	Homer and Herodotus, Prose Composition and Prosody.	Two Trigonometries, Mensuration, Surveying, Navigat'n, An'l Geometry, in part	Introductory and Popular Courses.
	Latin and Greek.	**Mathematics.**	**Metaphysics.**	**Natural Science.**
JUNIOR CLASS,	Tragedy and Comedy, Composition and Comp. Philology.	Analytical Geometry, Diff. and Integ. Calculus.	Mental Philosophy proper, Psychology, and Introductory Ethics.	Natural Philosophy, Mechanics (Silliman,) Astronomy (Loomis.)
	Latin and Greek.	**Metaphysics.**	**Natural Science.**	**Review**
SENIOR CLASS,	Tragedy, History, Literature and General Grammar.	Moral Philosophy, Logic, Rhetoric, Political Economy and Evidences of Christianity.	Chemistry, Mineralogy, and Geology and Natural History.	of Entire Course, for final Examinations and Graduation in Senior Year.

STEWART COLLEGE.

BIBLICAL COURSE THROUGH ALL THE COLLEGIATE CLASSES FOR FOUR YEARS.

JUNIOR CLASS.

FIRST TERM.

Horace, Epistles; Cicero de Oratore. · · ·
Gorgias of Plato, · · · · · Woolsey.
Rhetoric, · · · · · · Jamieson.
Greek and Latin Exercises, · · ·
Mechanics. · · · · · · ·

SECOND TERM.

Tacitus, Germania and Agricolo. · · ·
Antigone of Sophocles, · · · Woolsey.
Select Latin, Select Greek, or Modern Languages, at the option
   of the student.
Natural Philosophy, · · · · · Lardner.
Chemistry—Lectures and Experiments, · · Fownes.

SENIOR CLASS.

FIRST TERM.

Cicero's Tusculan Questions. · · · ·
Demosthenes de Corona, · · · · Champlin.
Mental Philosophy, · · · · · Upham.
Mineralogy, · · · · · · Dana.
Astronomy, · · · · · · ·
Meteorology, · · · · · Brocklesby.

SECOND TERM.

Logic, · · · · · · · Jamieson.
Political Economy, · · · · · Say.
Moral Philosophy, · · · · Wayland.
Evidences of Christianity, · · · Alexander.
Geology, · · · · · · St. John.
Zoology, · · · · · Agassiz & Gould.

   N. B.—Anthon's Classical Dictionary and Grecian and Roman Antiquities should be used as Books of Reference throughout the whole course. Exercises in elocution and composition by the classes in turn every Friday afternoon.

Today's curriculum must balance the powerful ideas of the past with the technology of the future.

though, was the introduction of a course in the Bible—required of all students for all four years.

With the change of the school's name in 1879 to Southwestern Presbyterian University came the first major restructuring of the curriculum. Following a trend noted in a few colleges across the country, the new program offered much more freedom of choice to the individual student.

According to Rhodes historian James E. Roper, "The reorganization of 1879 abolished once and for all the glorified-high-school approach to learning which had been in effect since 1848 and was still the prevalent system nationally. In accordance with modernized ideas on education, eight 'coordinate schools' were set up, each including several departments.

"These were the School of Ancient Languages (Latin, Greek); the School of Mathematics (Pure, Applied); the School of Philosophy (Mental Philosophy and Logic, Ethics, Political Economy); the School of Modern Languages (French, German, Spanish); the School of History and English (History, Literature, Rhetoric, Elocution, Composition); the School of Biblical Instruction (Bible Proper, Hebrew, New Testament Greek); the School of Commercial Science (Bookkeeping, Commercial Law, Penmanship, Drawing)."

Depending on the kind of degree being pursued, the student was required to graduate from three or four of the coordinate schools and demonstrate proficiency in several other subjects as well.

This system of coordinate schools gave way in 1909 to a simple listing of "courses of study" by departments, very similar to today's "courses of instruction." In 1918, a mixture of required courses and electives leading to majors was instituted, and it is this basic pattern that still structures the student's choices.

The elements that compose this pattern—the subjects, majors, and methods of teaching—have varied dramatically over the years. Some subjects have disappeared from catalogues; many, many more have been added. The traditional classroom and laboratory sessions are now but a few of the many forms and settings for teaching. The curriculum of this college has always reflected the world around it, and like the responsible institutions of that world, it has sought to honor what is valuable from the past even as it welcomed courageous new ideas.

Mind-to-Mind Contact:
The Tutorial Reading Course

Professor Margaret Townsend and her student discuss a weekly reading assignment.

In February 1922, in his plans for the new campus to be built in Memphis, President Diehl announced: "Inasmuch as the English system of higher education is, in our judgment, incomparably better for the moral welfare of the student than the Continental system, we propose as nearly as we can to follow the English system, with such modifications and adaptations as seem wise."

Diehl was speaking of the small individual colleges of Oxford and Cambridge, formed around cozy quadrangles, where students and faculty could live, dine, and study together. But it was more than the physical arrangements of Oxford and Cambridge that enchanted him. It was also the personal, one-on-one contact between professor and student in the tutorial classes that impressed him. And he was determined, with the aid of his cadre of English-trained faculty, to be one of the first American colleges to offer such classes.

In 1931 he accomplished his goal. With the aid of a grant from the Carnegie Foundation, tutorial reading courses were introduced into the curriculum. As Diehl reported after the first year of operation, "The plan is not so much a system as it is the humanizing and liberalizing of the student's work. As carried out, it provides that each student taking such a course shall do both intensive and extensive reading in some field of knowledge, and that he shall meet weekly with his professor for individual conference and direction."

Dr. Diehl would no doubt be pleased to know that the innovative tutorial courses are still a part of the Rhodes College tradition, and that the mind-to-mind contact he envisioned continues to stimulate both students and teachers in directed inquiries, internships, and honors tutorials.

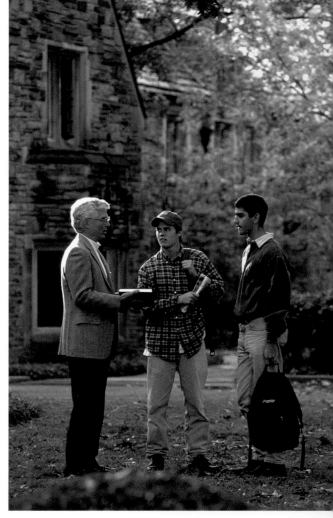

"Search" course instructor Robert Llewellyn continues the discussion after class with students.

Four of the five founders of the "Man" course (left to right): Kinney, Osman, Davis, Kelso.

Vanderbilt University Press published in 1996 an excellent account of the birth, development, and continuing evolution of the "Man/Search" course edited by Professor Michael Nelson, a member of the course's faculty, with contributions by Nelson and several instructors in the course.

"The defining academic experience at Rhodes College": The "Man/Search" Course

The need for a broad survey course based on Judeo-Christian values had been on Dr. Diehl's mind for a long time, but the horror of World War II brought it to the forefront. Along with many others, Dr. Diehl felt more and more that a liberal education, "concerned with convictions and consciences, with ultimate values," could help prevent the destruction of our civilization by the forces of ignorance and inhumanity. He pressed these views at every opportunity to his faculty and to the community at large. In 1945, his dream came true.

Professor W.R. Cooper, one of the creators, described the beginning:

"As a result of a critical study of the liberal arts curriculum by the entire faculty, and inspired by the sound counsel and guidance given to the members of the faculty by Professor Theodore M. Greene of Princeton on his visits to the Southwestern campus, an integrated course in the Humanities was introduced by them into the Southwestern curriculum in September, 1945. The working out of a syllabus for this course on 'Man in the Light of History and Religion' was largely the work of Professor A.P. Kelso, chairman of the committee of five professors (Professors A.P. Kelso and John Osman of the Philosophy Department, Professors W.R. Cooper and J.H. Davis of the History Department, and Professor Laurence Kinney of the Bible Department), who assumed responsibility for the teaching of the course. An effort was made 'to work the vast materials of our Western cultural heritage into an ordered whole under the integrating principles of history and religion.' A special reading room was set aside and equipped with the books and charts necessary for the 'Man' students, who met with their professors on three days each week to attend a lecture given by one of the professors, and who met in small conference sections on the other three days each week, with one of the five professors conducting each section."

Dr. Cooper also notes that the unprecedented amount of reading and study required of the "Man" students either stimu-

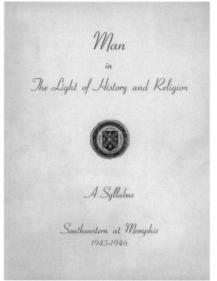

The syllabus for the first session of the "Man" course

lated them or overwhelmed them. He quotes one struggling freshman's statement about the experience of "Man": "If it takes five learned professors to teach this course, I don't see how one poor freshman can be expected to pass it."

Fifty-two years later, the thousands of students who have passed through the course would also say that it was their most valuable college experience. Professor Michael Nelson, a present-day instructor in the course, calls it "the defining academic experience at Rhodes College, the soul of the college in some ways."

In its first half-century, the course has never been static. The changing syllabus has reflected the different minds who assembled it. The manner of teaching has changed, the texts explored have changed, even the name has changed—in 1986 "Man" became "The Search for Values in the Light of Western History and Religion" or "Search" for short. And in that new name can be found the source of the course's continuing strength, for it encapsulates the idea of a liberal arts education, a never-ending exploration of who we are and how we got that way.

The innovative path created by the "Search" course has guided a number of other institutions. It has served as a model for similar courses at Davidson College, Hampden-Sydney College, Millsaps College, St. Andrews College, Austin College, Eckerd College, and the University of the South in Sewanee.

Perhaps most important, it has been emulated elsewhere in the Rhodes curriculum. The experience of bringing together faculty from several departments into a single course has led to interdisciplinary courses that draw on a number of resources to create wide-ranging programs in urban studies, American studies, Asian studies, and women's studies, among others.

Professor Greene of Princeton, the consultant on the original course in 1946, called it "one of the most significant educational projects in America." It is certainly one of this College's proudest and most enduring achievements.

The English Connection: British Studies at Oxford

The first group of Southwestern at Oxford students prepares to embark, June 17, 1970. Professor Clifton stands proudly at the center of his charges.

The handsome posters announcing each year's British Studies offerings are frequently framed.

SOUTHWESTERN AT OXFORD

Given the influence of Dr. Diehl and the Oxford-trained members of his faculty, it is somewhat surprising that it was not until 1970 that the College officially arranged a program that would fully expose its students to education in the English manner.

During a research project at Oxford in the summer of 1967, Yerger Clifton, Professor of English and a graduate of Trinity College in Dublin, conceived of a plan whereby he would bring his students from Memphis to England for a five-week immersion in English history. The students would live in the ancient quadrangles of Oxford, and classes would be taught by a combination of outstanding teachers from English universities and their home institution.

Dr. Clifton's plan became Southwestern at Oxford, which convened its first session at University College, Oxford in 1970. Two years later, the College broadened the sponsorship of the program to include a consortium of other Southern colleges and universities, changing the name of the program to British Studies at Oxford.

Today the summer program is housed at St. John's College, but the format is much the same as it was at the beginning: lectures, seminars, and workshops, plus visits to museums, important historical locations, and architectural landmarks. Classes are still taught by professors from English academia and the colleges of the consortium. The period of history to be studied varies each summer, so that over four years a broad view of English history is presented.

The World Is a Rhodes Classroom

Today the Rhodes campus knows no boundaries. A wide variety of study opportunities for undergraduates includes language programs in France, Russia, Spain, and Mexico; Greek and Roman studies in Greece; coral reef ecology and service training in Honduras; exchange programs in Belgium, France, Germany, Japan, Northern Ireland, Scotland, South Africa, and Spain; and two South American programs in Argentina and Chile.

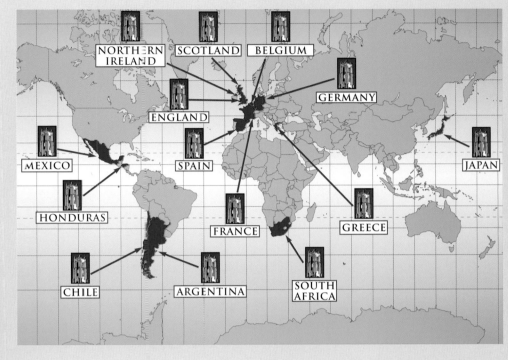

NORTHERN IRELAND · SCOTLAND · BELGIUM · GERMANY · ENGLAND · MEXICO · SPAIN · JAPAN · HONDURAS · FRANCE · GREECE · CHILE · ARGENTINA · SOUTH AFRICA

"Among Presbyterians learning and religion go hand in hand."

The stained-glass images of Mary and Martha in the Williams Prayer Room in Voorhies Hall were crafted by Charles Connick of Boston, one of America's premier stained-glass artists.

SAINT MARTHA
OF BETHANY

Bellingrath Hall includes a small chapel for prayer and meditation.

In his estimable history of the first 100 years of the College, Professor W. Raymond Cooper succinctly expressed the foundation of the relationship between this college and the church:

"It had long been the boast of the Presbyterian Church that among Presbyterians learning and religion go hand in hand, and that the history of Presbyterianism in any section is largely also an educational history of that region."

When the Synod of Nashville took over the foundering Montgomery Masonic College in 1855 and renamed it Stewart College, it needed make no radical changes to transform it into a church college. Dr. John T. Hendrick, minister of the Presbyterian Church in Clarksville, was already a member of the faculty, teaching Mental and Moral Science and Belles Lettres. He simply added to the curriculum Evidences of Christianity and a daily chapel requirement.

And when President William Stewart went fundraising for the young school he stated his priorities clearly:

"The amount to be raised will place the College on that elevated position of usefulness in the church and in the world which will be her glory and enable her as a true 'good mother' to open her religious education considerably."

Under the leadership of President John Shearer in 1870, a Biblical Course was inaugurated, a four-year program covering "Old and New Testament History, Archaiology [sic], Types, Laws, Fulfilled Prophecies [sic], the Unity of the Scriptures, and the Internal Evidences of Christianity." Furthermore, this course was required of all students. It was felt at the time, and has been claimed ever since, that this college was the first to institute such a required course in a non-seminary educational framework.

In the first year of his presidency Shearer stated his view of the role of religion in the classroom:

"The great question is: How shall we sanctify a secular education? Church institutions have hitherto failed to solve it, relying on the overshadowing influences of a mere denominationalism. Give us time and we propose to lay the foundations of an intelligent faith in the God of Nature and of Revelation as one and the same God. There is no need that the tendencies of scholastic studies be rationalistic, nor that the tendencies of science be atheistic or even un-Christian. Science and revelation should be woven in the same web. The foundations of faith should be laid every day in the classroom, and the entire harmony and unity of all truth should be the first and last lesson in every Christian school."

Later Dr. John N. Waddel, when accepting the chancellorship in 1879 of the school, summed up another point of enduring policy when he declared that "there is no need for the perpetual inculcation of theological dogma, but the religious needs of the student can best be insured by providing that the teachers employed be Christian men who by the silent influence of their daily life shall inculcate the principles of the Christian religion."

It was under Waddel that the College made the strongest expression of its connection to the church—first, with its new name, Southwestern Presbyterian University; and second, by instituting in 1885 a School of Theology, a professional school to prepare students for the ministry.

Although the School of Theology was closed in 1917 for financial reasons, Christianity has remained at the center of the College's operation. The College's mission statement says:

Rhodes' purpose is to serve God by:
• helping students to lead lives of genuineness and excellence,
• expanding the horizons of knowledge and scholarship, and
• living as a community of truth, loyalty and service in an atmosphere of academic freedom, open inquiry, and freedom of expression for all.

It is the policy of the College that requirements for graduation include two years of study of the Bible or Bible-related courses.

And President Daughdrill has made abundantly clear just how valid and necessary a religious college is in the last years of the twentieth century:

"The Christian college reconciles academic freedom with Christian commitment. At many universities the concepts seem mutually exclusive—the search for truth wherever it may lead seems to oppose a creedal faith. The church-related

"The great Apostle of God's law": Benjamin Morgan Palmer

On New Year's Day, 1901, three weeks before his eighty-third birthday, Rev. Benjamin Morgan Palmer preached what was later termed his Century Sermon from the pulpit of First Presbyterian Church, New Orleans, the church he had served since 1856.

One of the most revered men in New Orleans, honored and respected by all elements of the community, Palmer preached that day "at the request of prominent citizens irrespective of creed," according to a contemporary newspaper account. The newspaper further reported: "During the solemn address, the clock in the rear of the church ticked audibly. No one moved. No one spoke. No one whispered. There was not even the slightest coughing so common in densely crowded halls on damp days. When the great Apostle of God's law had finished, a gray-haired parishioner turned to the man at his elbow and said with strange earnestness and sincerity, measuring every word he uttered: 'Greatest man alive'."

Few in that crowd would have disagreed. Contemporary accounts of his sermons suggest that Palmer was a spellbinder of the first magnitude. After a famous—and successful—speech in opposition to the Louisiana State Lottery, a distinguished Jewish New Orleanian said: "It did not seem to me that it was Palmer who was speaking. He spoke as one inspired. It seemed to me that God Almighty was speaking through Palmer."

Palmer was born in Charleston, South Carolina, on January 25, 1818. After two years of study at Amherst, he transferred to the University of Georgia, where he graduated in 1838. He completed his studies at Columbia Theological Seminary in South Carolina and was licensed to preach in 1841. In 1856 he was called to First Church in New Orleans, where he remained until his death.

During the Civil War, Palmer served as a chaplain in the army of General Albert Sidney Johnson. When the yellow-fever epidemics of 1858 and 1878 struck New Orleans, prompting many residents to flee the city, Palmer remained to minister to the sick and dying of all faiths. In a letter to a friend during the 1878 epidemic, he wrote, "During three months, I paid each day from 30 to 50 visits, praying at the bedside of the sick, comforting the bereaved, and burying the dead."

Deeply committed to furthering the church's role in education, Palmer was the principal and most eloquent supporter of the idea of a Presbyterian university for the Southwest. As related elsewhere (Chapter One, the History of the College), he was offered the chancellorship of Southwestern Presbyterian University in 1874, but his congregation would not let him leave. Nevertheless, he continued as a powerful influence on the affairs of the University, serving on the Board of Directors from 1875-1901.

In 1921 the campaign to raise money for the College's new campus in Memphis received a major boost when the citizens of New Orleans, almost twenty years after Palmer's death, subscribed $200,000 to build Palmer Hall in fitting tribute to this dedicated disciple of Christian education.

Young Ministerial Students Much In Demand Around Memphis For Sermon

Call On Southwestern Boys To Take Pulpits In Absence of Regular Church Pastors

Maybe you didn't know it, but Southwestern is developing a group of young parsons that is already in great demand not only in Memphis, but even outside the state. Every Sunday these young men carefully brush their shoes, neatly part their hair, ascend the pulpit, and with fiery invective attack the evils of the present day. The Ministerial Club has done exceptionally fine work this year, both in supplying pulpits and in deputation service.

EMPLOY RADIO

The latest venture upon which the club has launched is a monthly-sponsored program of religious dramas to be given over W N B R. If plans newly adopted by "Camel" Cabaniss, who is strongly suspected by his fellow members of having views savoring of Romanism, do not miscarry, these programs will terminate in a series of the early mystery and miracle plays so popular in England before and during the Elizabethan Age. Cabaniss has quite liberally decided, however, that it might be best to give these plays in their English translations instead of in the original Latin.

GREGORY LEADS

But to return to the pulpit work of the Ministerial Club. James Gregory tops the list with four sermons to his credit so far this year. He has been heard at the Westminster, Court Avenue, and Parkview Presbyterian churches, and at the Mount Pisgah Methodist. Paul Jones has led prayer meeting at the Parkview Presbyterian, and James Breazeale has delivered sermons at McLemore Ave. Presbyterian and at Campbell's Clinic.

The Sou'wester,
February 19, 1932

sequent series of regional consultations led by the participants of the original study followed in 1998. These discussions are expected to yield a book of interest and value to all church-related colleges as they move into the twenty-first century. The entire project is yet more evidence of the devotion this college has to its Christian commitment and religious identity.

college does not exclude either but holds them in tension. I think this is a tremendous contribution to the church. The church, if it errs at all, errs on the anti-intellectual side, seeming at times in history to fear the discovery of new things. The fear of the Lord is the beginning of wisdom, but thinking new thoughts and making new discoveries leads to a first-hand philosophy, a firsthand faith, a firsthand theology. To worship God means no less than to think, and to think does not mean to parrot."

In the fall of 1995, with the backing of the Lilly Endowment, Inc., Rhodes initiated and hosted the Consultation on the Future of the Church-Related College. The College brought ten outstanding scholars from church-related colleges across the country and across the religious spectrum in a series of meetings to reflect on the challenges and opportunities facing such colleges today. A sub-

The brochure for the Rhodes Consultation on the Future of the Church-Related College displays the Bible surrounded by the heraldic symbols of the seven liberal arts, symbolizing the College's commitment to higher education in a Christian frame of reference.

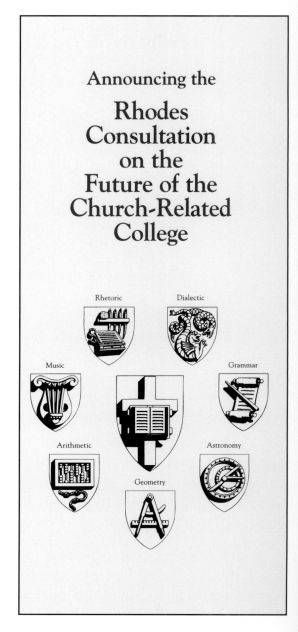

Announcing the

Rhodes Consultation on the Future of the Church-Related College

"At the ringing of the College Bell, the Professors and students shall assemble in the Chapel for prayers and roll call."

—Montgomery Masonic College catalogue, 1853-54

From its earliest days, the College expected every student to attend a daily chapel service to start the academic day. Chancellor Waddel described the services in the 1880s thusly:

"The Bible was read and prayer offered. We called no roll, but the students were distributed into classes of ten, and each class, with its own monitor, furnished with a card, on which were written the names of his class of ten, and his sole duty was to note absentees, and hand his card on Saturday morning to the presiding officer, and receive a new card for the ensuing week. Hymn-books also were distributed among the students, and it was really enjoyable to be present at prayers on account of the music, in which the large body of them engaged, with perfect decorum."

The catalogue of Southwestern Presbyterian University for 1897-98 stated clearly:

"Attendance at church at least once on each Sunday, daily attendance at Chapel, and attendance upon a Sunday Bible Class are required of all students. It has needed but little effort to secure these.

The great body of the students are earnest, faithful Christians and manly piety is at a premium in the institution."

But by the mid-1960s, the "manly piety" of the College's students called for less restrictive forms of worship. According to historian James Roper:

"In the fall of 1966, a student poll rejected the idea of requiring chapel attendance, by a two-thirds majority. The administration took its own poll of 19 Presbyterian ministers in the Memphis area, and found that 11 supported the students, feeling that compulsion 'cheapens the worship service,' that 'pressuring does not produce a worshipful attitude,' and that 'the school doesn't have the right to act as parent.'" A second major reason for the cessation of daily chapel was purely physical. As enrollment had increased, Hardie Auditorium was no longer able to hold the entire student body—nor was any other indoor meeting space on the campus.

In 1968 the administration announced that chapel attendance was no longer mandatory, though regular programs were offered on a voluntary basis.

The Presidential Pulpit

One clear indicator of the close relationship between Rhodes College and the church is the number of its presidents who have been ordained ministers. From the first preacher-president, Rev. R.B. McMullen, to the present incumbent, ten of the College's eighteen full-time presidents have been ministers of the Presbyterian Church. They are:

R.B. McMullen, 1859-62
J.B. Shearer, 1870-79
John N. Waddel, 1879-88
Charles C. Hersman, 1888-91
James M. Rawlings, 1891-92
George Summey, 1892-1903
Neander M. Woods, 1905-08
Charles E. Diehl, 1917-49
John David Alexander, 1965-69
James Harold Daughdrill, Jr., 1973-

Most of these presidents used the pulpit to promote the school whenever possible. When Diehl accepted the presidency, for example, one of his requests from the Board was an increase in travel allowance, which he promised to use to preach at every church in the supporting synods, appealing for funds and recruiting students.

The School of Theology, 1885-1917

"The diligence and faithfulness of these young brethren . . ."

This room was the meeting hall of the Palmer Homiletic Society, where members gathered weekly. According to the yearbook of 1899:

"The purpose of the society is to develop the practical side of the divinity student; for this purpose the programme of each week is carefully carried out. It consists of a sermon of 15 minutes, in which the student is not allowed to use notes; thus training him to deliver his sermons in after life without them.

"The second feature of the evening is an essay upon some practical subject, as 'The Minister's Functions,' 'The Pastor in the Sunday-school,' etc. After the essay is read, the subject is open for general discussion, each member expressing his opinions and suggesting points and methods not brought out.

"The third feature is the Homiletic address. This address is for 10 minutes and is almost entirely upon the subjects that have been studied in Systematic Theology. After the homilist has given his exposition upon the subject the members then have the privilege of general discussion."

When the School of Theology was established at Southwestern Presbyterian University in 1885, it was an action both predictable and rare: predictable in that the sponsoring churches might have been expected to ask that their college offer professional training for ministerial students; rare in that divinity courses were usually offered in seminary settings, where all the students were future ministers.

But Chancellor Waddel and his faculty seem to have felt that mixing secular and religious students would work to the advantage of both groups. It was hoped that the would-be ministers might have a salutary effect on the behavior of the more worldly students, and that contact with the secular students would prepare the religious students for their future work in the world.

The divinity students, called "theologues," were housed in Robb Hall on the campus, while all other students were required to board with approved families in Clarksville, where they could benefit from "the culture and restraints of a home circle."

Although most seminaries at that time offered a three-year course, the SPU administration felt that the necessary work could be done in only two years. The success of their graduates would seem to bear that out. The SPU Journal of May 1894 reports on the success of the senior divinity students who appeared before the Nashville Presbytery that spring, where the Presbytery passed a resolution recording its "deep and thankful sense of the value of the method of training and of the ability of the instructors in our Theological School at Clarksville, where these young men were prepared for their work."

The Nashville Presbytery also expressed its "hearty appreciation of the diligence and faithfulness of these young brethren in their preparatory studies, and of the fine promise they give of efficiency in the ministry."

But by 1917, it had become obvious to the Synods that there were now more seminaries than the church needed or could pay for. Therefore, in order to preserve SPU as a liberal college of arts and sciences, the trustees decided to accept the resolution of Dr. William M. Alexander that "Because of the present financial condition of the Southwestern Presbyterian University, and the impracticality of raising sufficient funds for its necessities during the general unsettlement of the country on account of the war, the Theological School be suspended."

The members of the Homiletic Society in 1909

The "benevolent spirit" of the Theology School: Joseph Wilson

The Scotch Enlightenment, a Protestant strain derived from the University of Edinburgh in its classic age, has been praised by the contemporary scholar J.D. Hoeveler for "its cultivation of reasonableness, its obsession with social and civic virtue, its concern for improvement and faith in progress, its confidence in human nature and its generally benevolent spirit."

It is a description that perfectly suits the man brought to Clarksville by Chancellor Waddel in 1885 to teach theology, Dr. Joseph Ruggles Wilson.

Born in 1822 in Steubenville, Ohio, he was the youngest son of Judge James Wilson, owner of newspapers in Steubenville and in Pittsburgh, Pennsylvania. He graduated from Jefferson College in Canonsburg, Pennsylvania, and attended Princeton Theological Seminary. In 1849 he married Jessie Woodrow, the daughter

of a Presbyterian minister in Chillicothe, Ohio, and two weeks later was ordained in that same faith himself.

After five years teaching rhetoric, chemistry, and natural science at Hampden-Sydney College, he was called to his first pastorate in Staunton, Virginia, in 1855. The following year Jessie Wilson presented her husband with his first son, named Thomas Woodrow in honor of her brother and destined to be the twenty-eighth President of the United States.

The young family was soon on the move again; in 1858 Joseph Wilson was called to the ministry of First Presbyterian Church in Augusta, Georgia, where he remained during the Civil War.

Although he had been born in Union territory, Wilson aligned himself with the cause of his adopted South. After the Southern Presbyterian Synods withdrew from the General Assembly of the Church in Philadelphia in May 1861, Wilson invited them to meet in Augusta to form their own assembly. When the meeting was held in his church the following December, he was elected recording clerk and Dr. Benjamin Palmer was named moderator.

From 1870 to 1874, Wilson was professor of pastoral theology at Columbia Theological Seminary in Columbia, South Carolina. In 1874 he became minister of First Presbyterian Church in Wilmington, North Carolina, where he remained until he came to Clarksville.

From the way August Hecksher, Woodrow Wilson's biographer, describes the elder Wilson, it is easy to see why he was such a beloved member of the faculty: "His preaching was a blend of learning and of direct, almost blunt communication, his phrases tuned and honed until they struck close to the heart of everyday concerns. His theology, emphasizing the less intimidating aspects of Calvinism, promoted a geniality that spread into his daily life. He was full of humor. Loving the play of words, he seemed to be bursting in his prime with zest and self-confidence. He acted as if conversation were a chief end of life and puns one of its major diversions. He enjoyed billiards and was not averse to taking a nip of whisky—good Scotch whisky—now and then."

Wilson's public lectures at SPU always drew a full house. An observer at his lecture entitled "Courage"—given for the benefit of the University gymnasium in October 1886—reported, "His intermingling of wit and wisdom, jest and judgment, pleasantry and pathos, evinced a master's hand."

At the age of seventy, Wilson retired from teaching and did further service as a relief clergyman in several churches. In 1901, his ill health made it necessary for him to move in with Woodrow, the son of whom he was so proud, then a professor at Princeton. It was there that he died in 1903, after seeing his much-loved son inaugurated as President of Princeton.

The Heresy Trial of Charles E. Diehl

"Unsound in the Faith"

It began with an unhappy employee, Dr. W.S. Lacy. For seven years Lacy had served as Executive Secretary of the College. He resigned in August 1930, nursing a resentment that Diehl had not offered him a faculty position teaching Bible. On September 30 he wrote Diehl a long, strongly worded letter denouncing the President for using "the influence which your position gives you to weaken faith in the Scriptures."

Diehl replied on October 2 with a blistering point-by-point denial of Lacy's charges that concluded, "Your letter is the most astounding and disappointing thing that has come my way, and the future can hold no greater shocks."

He was wrong. Greater shocks were to come. On the evening of October 3, four local Presbyterian ministers, urged on by Lacy, appeared unexpectedly in Diehl's office and requested him to resign for three reasons: the unsoundness of his faith, the recklessness of his financial administra-

tion, and his unchurchly acceptance of student dances on campus. Diehl declined to resign, and told them to do what they pleased with their petition.

Accordingly, a petition dated October 6, 1930, and signed by eleven ministers of the Memphis Presbytery was sent to the Board of Trustees. It charged:

1. *That the President of the college is not what may be called "Sound in the Faith," that he disbelieves in the full inspiration of the Scriptures, and does not adhere to many of the teachings of the Standards of the Presbyterian Church in the United States.*

2. *That the President of Southwestern is a reckless administrator in the handling of the funds belonging to the college.*

3. *That it is our belief that the Presbyterian constituency of Memphis has lost confidence in the administration of the President of the college.*

The charge of permitting dancing had

The St. Louis Post-Dispatch compared the Diehl trial to the 1925 trial in Dayton, Tennessee, where schoolteacher John Scopes was convicted of teaching the theory of evolution. The photograph of the pajama party was a creation of the newspaper, designed to spice up the story with a little leg art.

ANOTHER HERESY HUNT IN TENNESSEE

Dr. Charles E. Diehl, President of Southwestern College, Charged With Questioning the Bible and Allowing Pajama Parties, But So Far He Has Held the Fort Against His Enemies.

apparently been replaced by the "loss of confidence" accusation. But the dancing charge continued to be talked of, since it stated rather sensationally that there had been "pajama parties" on campus with female students dressed in abbreviated costumes.

The charges were repeated in a meeting of the Presbyterian Pastors Association on December 22, when the ministers who had signed the petition urged other ministers to speak out. This meeting and the content of the petition were reported in the press, causing both Memphis newspapers to editorialize in Dr. Diehl's behalf. The wire services quickly spread the charges around the country.

Obviously, the Board of Trustees had to take some action. So they requested the petitioning ministers to present their case to the Board on February 3.

Presided over by the Honorable Watkins Overton, Mayor of Memphis, the meeting began with a request from the petitioners that reporters be barred from the session, since "the newspapers are against us." The request was denied. The Board had decided that all transactions would be fully reported and had even hired its own court stenographer to record the proceedings.

Dr. J.P. Robertson then presented a lengthy list of ways in which Diehl failed to adhere to the standards of the church, including not believing in the history or science of the first part of Genesis; not accepting the imprecatory Psalms as of God; stating that the Shorter Catechism was "pedagogically unsound"; and holding no set theory of atonement.

The financial recklessness charges included indignation at the expenditure of $400 for a bulletin board, $200 for street signs "which had no meaning," and $1,400 for monogrammed dishes.

In response, Diehl presented a prepared statement in which he defined his idea of a Christian college: "Truth is found only by those who with open mind and honest heart, reverently and humbly and persistently seek it . . . The idea of determining by a vote of a church court the sort of theory, theological, ecclesiastical, political, social or economic, which is to be held and taught in a Christian college is the height of absurdity."

The Board then accepted a declaration in support of Dr. Diehl signed by every member of the faculty except one and a resolution "enthusiastically endorsed by the student body" expressing absolute confidence in his policies.

A large sheaf of letters in support of Diehl included communications from civic leaders, educators, Presbyterian ministers, businessmen, and alumni.

After proper consideration of the charges against Diehl and the evidence presented, the Board unanimously concluded:

"We feel that this investigation has not only completely vindicated him from every charge made, but has presented fresh and convincing demonstration of the vast value of his services to the cause of Christian education."

The Battle of Pamphlets

Pamphlets issued by both sides of the heresy conflict kept the discussion alive for three years after the trial.

Memphis, Tenn., March 20th, 1931.

NEEDED CHANGES IN SOUTHWESTERN COLLEGE

(An Address to the Ministers, Elders and Others of the Synods of Alabama, Louisiana, Mississippi and Tennessee.)

...inisters of Memphis filed a

More Light on Southwestern College

Memphis, Tenn., May 30, 1931

("The battle of pamphlets," as a papers, was begun by the Diehl. They on th

Southwestern at the Cross-Roads

FACTS
ABOUT THE
Southwestern Controversy

...and prepared by me without any ...d the entire expense of printing

...e an injustice. I have had Dr. ...ence before printing

August, 1934

An Appeal for More Real Religion

Memphis, Tenn., August, 1934

...and judgment."

June, 1934

THE CHURCH'S "LOST CAUSE"
OF "PURITY"
...ON OF FALSEHOOD)

"They I have long who defame I seemed to in admira

The Official Report of the Hearing of the Charges
Preferred By Eleven Presbyterian Ministers
Against President Charles E. Diehl
Held On Tuesday, February 3rd, 1931
By the Board of Directors of SOUTHWESTERN

...e Synod of Tenn., ...the Assem... ...t hear and ...y the Board

...mit:—
...court of first ...ls (Bk. of Ch. ...admit or con... ...es in the case."
...n evidence duly ...he provisions re... ...NGES apply to ...ary" because my ...resolution was laid

The Kinney Program

"With the privilege of education comes the responsibility of service."

—Dr. Laurence Kinney

Big Brother Darin Hornsby '94 shows Little Brother Joshua Austin around the Rhodes campus.

Dr. Larry Lacy '59 (on the ladder) worked with the Rhodes chapter of Habitat for Humanity in 1988.

The idea came from Dr. Laurence Kinney, professor of Bible and religion, and several of his colleagues in the Religion Department. In order "to strengthen still further the moral, spiritual and religious life of the . . . campus community," they proposed in 1956 a three-year, three-part project to the Danforth Foundation: to provide a more definitive vocational guidance program for students; to encourage Christian service projects for the students; and to encourage Christian perspectives in teaching for the faculty.

The student service project flourished like seeds in rich soil. Established as the Danforth Program in 1957, the name was later changed to honor the founder of the project. From the forty-five or so students who served in the first year, participation has increased to more than a thousand—an estimated seventy-five percent of today's 1,400-plus student body. Literally thousands of Rhodes students have given of themselves to others by way of the Kinney Program.

Students can choose from a list of over sixty projects serving a wide range of needs: hospitals, literacy, hunger and homelessness, youth guid-

ance, senior services, conservation, civil rights, and crisis services. Although most Kinney Volunteers give approximately three hours each week to their work, some special projects call for a much greater time commitment, such as the annual alternative spring break trip, when students travel to the Texas-Mexican border to help an impoverished community.

Rhodes Chaplain Billy Newton '74 administers the Kinney Program, with the help of a cadre of student coordinators. According to Newton, there have been discussions of making volunteer service a curriculum requirement. "But we decided against it. Students are serving by choice, why make it mandatory?"

Students have also initiated a number of projects, including the Rhodes campus chapter of Habitat for Humanity, one of the first college-sponsored Habitat chapters in the country; tutoring programs at nearby Snowden School; the Kinney Music Program for Kids, giving music lessons to children from low-income families; and Souper Contact, the soup kitchen operated by students at St. John's United Methodist Church every Tuesday of the year.

The value of the Kinney Program to the community and to the students who participate has been recognized by the alumni, friends, and foundations who have contributed to its support. The Bonner Foundation and the Day Foundation have created scholarship programs that provide stipends to students, freeing them from part-time jobs so they can work in community service.

Although the Kinney Program drew its inspiration from the Presbyterian tradition of service to the community as a form of Christian commitment, today it is entirely ecumenical. Approximately seventeen percent of Kinney volunteers are Presbyterian; the rest are representatives of several other Protestant denominations, Unitarians, Catholics, Jews, Hindus, Muslims, and even those of "no affiliation."

The windows of Frazier Jelke Science Center become a billboard for the varied activities of Kinney's Hunger & Homelessness Week.

Coordinator Kristen Miller '97 works with a pupil in the Kinney Music Program.

Service Opportunities through the Kinney Program

Hospitals and Health Care

Church Health Center
Le Bonheur Children's Hospital
Ronald McDonald House
St. Jude Children's Research Hospital
Veterans Medical Center

Literacy and Education

Memphis Literacy Council
Lester Reading Program
Time to Read Literacy Program
WYPL Talking Library

Snowden Adopt-a-School Program

Adopt-a-Friend Program
Kinney Creative Writing
Kinney Music for Kids
Reading Renaissance

Church-Related Ministries

Catholic Charities
Evergreen Children's Ministry
First Presbyterian Downtown Program
Hope Ministries Program
Neighborhood Christian Center
Streets Ministry
Young Life
Youth ministry in local churches

Hunger and Homelessness

Final Net Homeless Children
First Presbyterian Soup Kitchen
Habitat for Humanity
Memphis Family Shelter
Memphis Food Bank
MIFA Estival Place
MIFA Home Delivered Meals
Souper Contact Soup Kitchen

Disabilities and Independent Living

Center for Independent Living
Mid-South Association for Retarded Citizens
SRVS Residential and Vocational Service
Skinner Recreational Service
United Cerebral Palsy Center
YWCA-Martha's Manor

Children and Youth Guidance

Big Brothers/Big Sisters
Boys and Girls Club
Evergreen Afterschool Program
Porter Leath Children's Center
SMART Youth Program
VECA Youth Leadership Corps

Crisis Services and Special Needs

Aloysius House
Crisis Center of Memphis
Dismas House
Family Link
Friends for Life
Hope House (day care for HIV/AIDS)
YWCA Abused Women's Services
Youth Villages

Senior Services

Alzheimer's Day Care
St. Peter's Villa

Peace, Justice and Environment

Campus Green
CASA Court Appointed Advocates
Memphis Humane Society
Mid-South Peace and Justice Center
Wolf River Conservancy
Lichterman Nature Center
National Civil Rights Museum
VECA Neighborhood Initiative
Gandhi Institute for Non-Violence

Special Events and One-Time Projects

Hands-On Memphis
Hunger and Homelessness Week
Orientation Service Plunge
National Youth Service Day

Special Projects and Commitments

Bonner Scholars
Heifer Project International
Kinney Community Interns
Service-Learning Fellows
Tex-Mex Border Ministry

"It was to be enduring . . .
It was to be beautiful . . .
It was to be genuine throughout . . ."

Chapter Six: The Campus

"Genuineness is characteristic of the heart of this institution, and we wanted this note sounded everywhere, even in the construction of the physical plant. It was to be enduring, for we were building for generations to come. It was to be beautiful, for the aesthetic side of man's nature is important and a college of liberal culture dare not overlook it. It was to be genuine throughout, free from all substitutions and cheap, make-believe effects, for this college has a hatred of sham. It is a source of satisfaction to know that our architectural ideal has been realized, and that not even the most caustic and unfriendly critic can now or hereafter indulge in a smile of derision at our expense."

—President Charles E. Diehl,
The Ideals of Southwestern

Gothic Is in the Details

The Lancet Window

Memphis architect Metcalf Crump, who designed Buckman, Blount, Robinson, and Hassell Halls, as well as the McCoy Theatre and the West Hall of the Burrow Refectory, notes of the Collegiate Gothic style: "There are so many variations in the detailing of the buildings ... more possibilities than you might find in modern architecture."

A stroll around the Rhodes campus will quickly demonstrate the truth of Crump's observations. In the best Gothic tradition, every building conforms to the overall style yet combines the elements of that style in myriad different ways. As a result, every building displays unique details that enliven it and create its own particular character. Herewith, a small sampling of the Gothic design vocabulary as seen on the Rhodes campus.

The Pinnacle Spire

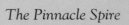

The Oriel Window (small)

The Oriel Window (medium)

The Oriel Window (large)

The Sphere

The Pointed Arch

A Variety of Arches

The Gargoyles of Rhodes

This grim-visaged likeness of Dr. Peyton Rhodes was carved in affectionate tribute by the stonecutters who enjoyed long-time employment on the many buildings erected during Dr. Rhodes' presidency. Legend has it that Dr. Rhodes, displeased with his depiction when it appeared high on the wall of Glassell, had it removed to his garden. But one of the stonecutters says that Rhodes' first concern was to remove a hazardous temptation from students who might want to climb up and decorate his face on certain occasions. It now grimaces benignly on the west wall of Blount Hall.

On the east face of the tower of the Bryan Campus Life Center, the gargoyle at far right bears a striking resemblance to President James Daughdrill.

87

The Buildings of Rhodes

Palmer Hall

The first completed building on the Memphis campus, Palmer Hall houses administrative offices, classrooms, and Hardie Auditorium. It was dedicated November 27, 1925, and honors the memory of Dr. Benjamin Morgan Palmer, a longtime trustee of this college and pastor of First Presbyterian Church, New Orleans.

Berthold S. Kennedy Hall

Called Science Hall when it was opened in 1925, this classroom building was remodeled in 1968 to house the Department of Chemistry and named in honor of alumnus Dr. Berthold S. Kennedy '12.

Hugh M. Neely Hall

The original dining hall on the Memphis campus, provided through the generosity of Mrs. Mary Sneed Neely in memory of her husband, Neely Hall is now a part of the dining complex called the Catherine Burrow Refectory.

Hubert F. Fisher Memorial Garden

Provided by Mrs. Hubert Fisher in honor of her husband, a United States congressman, the stone stage surrounded by an azalea garden has been the fair-weather setting for the College's commencement exercises since 1941.

Ashner Gateway

This gateway to the original core of the campus was given in memory of I.W. and Sallie Ashner by Mrs. Julius Goodman and Mrs. Ike Gronauer.

Robb Hall

The first residence hall on the Memphis campus bears the same name as the original dormitory in Clarksville, honoring Alfred Robb, a trustee who donated the land in Clarksville on which that dormitory was built.

Voorhies Hall

Provided by the generosity of Mrs. Emma Denie Voorhies, the first residence hall built for women on the campus was dedicated April 10, 1948. The Williams Prayer Room, an intimate chapel on the first floor, was given in memory of John Whorton and Anna Fletcher Williams by their children Sallie P. and Susan Fletcher Williams.

Frank M. Harris Memorial Building

The gate lodge was the home of physical plant supervisor John Rollow and his family in the '20s and '30s. It was later named the Frank M. Harris Memorial Building and now serves as the offices of the Alumni Program.

Hunt Gateway

A memorial to Captain William Ireys Hunt '34, this gateway to the campus from University Avenue was the gift of the First Presbyterian Church, Greenville, Mississippi, in 1948.

The Old Library

Before the construction of the Burrow Library, the library was located in this room on the third floor of Palmer Hall.

White Hall

Originally Calvin Hall, this residence hall was one of the first five Memphis buildings. In 1947 it was dedicated to the memory of Dr. Gordon White.

Burrow Library

Dedicated in 1953 in honor of Mr. and Mrs. A.K. Burrow and renovated in 1988, Burrow Library now houses more than 240,000 volumes, as well as a media center, the college archives, and the Walter P. Armstrong Rare Book Room.

William Neely Mallory Gymnasium

An active sportsman and one-time All-American, Mr. Mallory served the College as football coach, trustee, and treasurer. In 1945 he was killed in action in Italy. The gymnasium was dedicated in his honor in 1954.

Fargason Field House

Erected in 1928 as a temporary athletic facility, Fargason Field House continued in use until 1954. In the last basketball game played here, February 20, 1954, the Lynx defeated traditional rival Sewanee 66-64.

Catherine Burrow Refectory

By the 1950s, Neely Hall could no longer accommodate all the campus diners, so a new dining complex was planned around it. In 1958 the Catherine Burrow Refectory, honoring Mrs. A.K. Burrow, added considerable kitchen space and several dining areas: the Alburty Room, honoring Rhodes trustee E.A. Alburty; Hyde Hall, dedicated in 1993 in honor of Dr. Margaret Hyde '34, benefactor and trustee; the Davis Room, named to honor Thomas B. Davis of Memphis. West Hall, an additional dining space, was built in 1987.

Ellett Hall

Attached to White Hall, this residence hall was completed in 1956 and dedicated to the memory of Dr. E.C. Ellett of Memphis, Class of 1888.

Margaret Townsend Hall

Constructed as a residence hall for women, Townsend Hall was completed in 1961. Its name honors the memory of Margaret Huxtable Townsend, a member of the school's faculty from 1918 to 1954 and Dean of Women from 1925 to 1952.

Bellingrath Hall

Dedicated in 1961, this residence hall memorializes Dr. Walter D. Bellingrath of Mobile, Alabama, a longtime friend and benefactor of the College.

Gooch Hall

Adjoining Palmer Hall and the Richard Halliburton Memorial Tower, Gooch Hall houses the Office of the President and the offices of Student Affairs and the Academic Deans. Built in 1962, it was dedicated in 1981 in memory of Boyce Alexander and Cecil Milton Gooch.

Richard Halliburton Memorial Tower

Mr. and Mrs. Wesley Halliburton bestowed this landmark to the College in 1962 in memory of their son, the distinguished world traveler and author. The 140-foot tower houses a seven-foot-wide, four-ton iron bell—cast in France especially for the tower—that sounds the hours for the campus in a resonant A-flat.

Castle Plaque

A part of the College's first building in Clarksville in 1850, this marble plaque honoring the founding donors now rests on the south face of the tower.

Moore Moore Infirmary

Dr. Moore Moore, Sr., for many years the college physician, also served as secretary of the Board of Directors from 1925 until his death in 1957. The infirmary was made possible through a bequest of Dr. Moore as a memorial to his wife, Ethel Shirley Moore.

Thomas W. Briggs Student Center

In the center of the campus, the Briggs Student Center houses the campus bookstore, post office, social rooms, and student activity offices. Dedicated in 1966, it was made possible by gifts of Mr. and Mrs. Thomas W. Briggs, founder of Welcome Wagon, augmented by gifts from parents and other friends.

Suzanne Trezevant Hall

Built in 1960, this women's residence hall was given by Edward H. Little, retired board chairman of Colgate-Palmolive Corporation, in memory of his Memphis-born wife, Suzanne Trezevant Little.

Alfred C. Glassell Hall

Constructed in the shape of a "J" in order to preserve the priceless mature trees of the area, Glassell Hall is a men's residence hall dedicated in 1968 to the memory of Alfred C. Glassell '11, Shreveport, Louisiana, alumnus and longtime member of the Board of Trustees.

Anne Marie Caskey Williford Hall

Constructed in 1969, this residence hall for women was named in 1980 in memory of Anne Marie Williford, who was Dean of Women from 1968 to 1975, and Dean of Students from 1975 until her death in 1979.

Frazier Jelke Science Center

The innovative design of the Frazier Jelke Science Center places this building's classrooms, lecture halls, and laboratories underground. It was dedicated in 1968 in memory of Mr. Frazier Jelke of New York. The amphitheatre in front of the entrance hosts student assemblies and entertainments.

Ohlendorf Hall

Home of the Mathematics Department and the Buckman Library for Biology and Mathematics, Ohlendorf honors the many contributions to this college of Harold Ohlendorf '31, of Osceola, Arkansas.

Rhodes Tower

The top of Rhodes Tower sparkles with three silver domes containing telescopes and an optical tracker for the Physics Department. Downstairs are classrooms, offices, and laboratories for the Physics Department and foreign language offices. Its name honors Dr. Peyton Nalle Rhodes, Professor of Physics 1926-49 and President of the College 1949-65.

SOUTHWESTERN AT MEMPHIS
RECORDS ITS ARCHITECTURAL DEBT TO

HENRY C. HIBBS   H. CLINTON PARRENT, JR.
1882 - 1949   1902 - 1967
M. F. A., HONORIS CAUSA, '38   D. F. A., HONORIS CAUSA, '58

WHOSE VISION OF EXCELLENCE, FIDELITY OF DESIGN,
AND INTEGRITY OF EXECUTION
SET A PATTERN OF ACHIEVEMENT WHICH WILL CONTINUE
TO ENRICH THIS COLLEGE AND THE NATION WITH A HERITAGE
OF ENDURING BEAUTY AND USEFULNESS.

"WHEN WE BUILD, LET US THINK THAT WE BUILD FOR EVER."
JOHN RUSKIN

19 OCTOBER 1968

Hibbs/Parrent Plaque

This plaque in Frazier Jelke Science Center honors the two architects who designed all but one of the major buildings erected by the College between 1925 and 1968.

S. Dewitt Clough Hall

Clough Hall shelters a heterogeneous collection of scholars in anthropology/sociology, psychology and religious studies. The Art Department's classrooms and studios cluster congenially near the Clough-Hanson Gallery on the first floor. The hall was named in memory of S. Dewitt Clough of Chicago in 1970.

Alburty Swimming Complex

The pool and its sunning terrace were added to the campus in 1977 through the generosity of E.A. and Emily Alburty.

Ruth Sherman Hyde Gymnasium

In 1971, this addition to the Neely Mallory Gymnasium provided space for the development of women's athletic programs. It was made possible by gifts from the J.R. Hyde family.

McCoy Theatre

The former Zeta Tau Alpha sorority house was transformed in 1982 into a flexible theater space that permits arena, thrust, proscenium, or environmental staging. It was funded by a gift from the McCoy Foundation, established by Harry B. McCoy in memory of his parents, Minetry and Harry McCoy.

Robinson Hall

This residence hall, completed in 1985, also serves as one of the College's primary summer conference facilities. Its name honors the memory of James D. Robinson, Memphis business leader and founder of Auto-Chlor, Inc.

Hassell Hall

The Music Department received its new home in 1984 through the generosity of the Hassell family of Clifton, Tennessee, and other friends and alumni of the College. Along with the classrooms, practice rooms, and music library, the building contains the Shirley M. Payne Recital Hall, named in honor of a friend of the College.

Blount Hall

The College's newest residence hall, completed in 1986, was named in honor of two of the College's greatest friends and benefactors, Carolyn and Wynton M. Blount.

Spann Place

This complex of five townhouses was completed in 1987 and named for alumna Jeannette S. Spann. Each townhouse has space for six students, usually engaged in a common academic or other special project.

Dorothy King Hall

Originally built as the national headquarters of Pi Kappa Alpha fraternity, it was purchased by the College in 1988 and named for a longtime friend and benefactor. It now houses the Office of Development and the Meeman Center for Lifelong Learning.

Tuthill Hall

Formerly the home of the Music Department, Tuthill Hall is named for Dr. Burnet C. Tuthill, the College's first Professor of Music. Renovated in 1987, it serves as the campus activities center for student organizations and groups.

Buckman Hall

The home of a trio of departments, Buckman Hall is occupied by the International Studies, Economics and Business Administration, and Political Science faculty and staff. It also shelters the Computer Center, the Language Laboratory and the Wynton M. Blount Lecture Hall. The building was dedicated in 1991 in honor of Mertie W. Buckman and the late Stanley J. Buckman and their family, longtime and generous supporters of the College. The central tower is named in honor of President and Mrs. James H. Daughdrill, Jr. and was donated anonymously by an alumna-trustee.

Bryan Campus Life Center

The most ambitious construction project in the College's history, the new Center joins Mallory and Hyde gymnasiums to become the largest structure on campus. Major funding for the facility was provided by the four children of Catherine Wilkerson Bryan of West Point, Mississippi, and the Center bears her name. Included in the facility's spaces are a three-court multi-use gymnasium, racquetball and squash courts, fitness room, indoor jogging track, ballroom, reception hall, and the new Lynx Lair.

The L. Palmer Brown Lynx Lair

This student recreation area houses a snack bar, game rooms, televisions, and lounge areas—even room for informal class meetings.

The Virginia and Robert McCallum Ballroom

For formal banquets, dances, lectures and other assemblies.

The Multi-Purpose Gymnasium

Three basketball courts wide, this versatile hall can also be used for large campus assemblies, including an indoor commencement ceremony when necessary.

The Brenda and Lester Crain Reception Hall

For social gatherings of all kinds.

Postcards from the Campus

From the early days of picture postcards at the turn of the century through today, this college has been a favorite subject of postcard vendors in Clarksville and in Memphis.

ENTRANCE TO SOUTHWESTERN, "THE COLLEGE OF THE MISSISSIPPI VALLEY," MEMPHIS, TENN.—11

SOUTHWESTERN COLLEGE, MEMPHIS, TENNESSEE

The Richard Halliburton Memorial Tower Memphis, Tennessee

Palmer Hall, Southwestern College of the Mississippi Valley, Memphis, Tennessee

IWESTERN PRESBYTERIAN UNIVERSITY, CLARKSVILLE, TENN.

RHODES COLLEGE

635 Southwestern Presbyterian University, Clarksville, Tenn.

Just finished from Augusta — see postmark tomorrow M...

504 College
1/3/07

Stewart Hall, S.P.U. Clarksville, Tenn.

Photo. by Elbric

1676

SOUTHERN PRESBYTERIAN UNIVERSITY, CLARKSVILLE, TENN.

The 150th Anniversary celebration at Rhodes kicked off in
January 1998 with an all-campus party hosted by
Panhellenic, the campus organization which governs and
oversees the sorority system.

"... to lose oneself in generous enthusiasms and cooperate with others for common ends."
—William DeWitt Hyde

Almost from the start, students at the College have found reasons and avenues beyond the classroom for gathering with their peers. Whether the stated aim is to salute achievement, debate issues, provide avenues for socializing or outlets for community service, campus organizations have also answered students' needs to belong to a group or extended family.

Campus organizations also have given students the chance to lead and be led and to improve their skills at both. Such endeavors have taught them about cooperation and working toward a common goal.

Equally important, they have helped define the College itself. The culture of Rhodes is inextricably tied to the philosophy of student self-governance set in motion by Chancellor William Dinwiddie in the early 1900s with the formation of the Student Council "for the purpose of encouraging student initiative and student government on the campus."

Yell for Your State

State clubs were a feature on the campus at the turn of the century, and each club had its own yell.

Texas:	**Alabama:**	**Louisiana:**
Rah for Texas!	*Razzle! Dazzle!*	*Oyez! Oyez! zip, hoo, ah!*
Fun and noise!	*Hobble! Gobble!*	*Comme vous, portez vous!*
Sparks and Anderson!	*Zip! Boom! Bah!*	*Louisiana!*
"Thee" cowboys!	*Here we are!*	
	Here we are!	
	Alabama-a-a!	

Student Election Commission members check out candidates' ads in the 1950s.

Today more than eighty organizations exist on campus, scores of ways for the collegiate population to get involved. And if students cannot find an organization that fits their interests, it is simple enough to create one that does. Many of the organizations that have emerged over the years originated in the mind of a single student.

In the College's earliest years, the list of organizations was short, dominated by the literary societies. By the 1920s, however, an eclectic group of organizations had emerged: the Sanhedrin, intended to oversee the activities of freshmen; the YMCA; the Nitists, a club of faculty and students who met to discuss issues; an orchestra and a glee club; a booster's club to support the welfare of the student body; and state clubs like the Alabama Club and the Texas Club, remembered for their distinctive state yells.

Various honorary fraternities emerged as well, their purposes tied to recognizing scholarship or literary achievement. The collegiate sense of humor was also evident in extracurricular life as early as 1919 with the formation of the Hankshaws, a short-lived group whose aim it was "to lead weak and tempted freshmen to see the charms of life, of dissipation and idleness." The *Sou'wester* listed a few of the membership requirements:

"Six cups of coffee a day . . . the constant use of tobacco in some form (snuff alone being prohibited) . . . the use of taxis for all distance exceeding two blocks . . . an average of three loafing nights a week . . ."

The colonization of the College's first fraternity, Pi Kappa Alpha, occurred in 1878. In 1921, a group of women students petitioned the national Chi Omega sorority for a chapter, hoping "the location of a sorority here will make the school more attractive to the other girls who consider going away to college." The following year that chapter was established. The Greek system grew to five national fraternities and two sororities by the time the College moved to Memphis in 1925. Today there are six fraternities and seven sororities, including two historically black sororities.

The Philosophy Club, begun in 1919, was the College's first co-ed club. The Women's Undergraduate Society, founded a decade later, was the first organization established to promote women's welfare on campus. The Black Student Association, established in 1969-70, was the first organization to promote what one Lynx yearbook of the 1990s describes as "harmonious relationships among people of different cultures and backgrounds."

The 1960s and '70s saw the emergence of more politically-oriented organizations like the Arts Renaissance Group—ARG for short—which "combined protest with good humor by conducting a 'war weekend' featuring fun and games along with anti-war programs," according to Professor Jim Roper's 1975 history of the College.

Since the 1920s students have faced a multitude of options for involvement—so many options that campus leaders have, at times, sought to minimize the risk of extracurricular overextension. In 1935, Omicron Delta Kappa, the national honorary leadership fraternity, inaugurated a "student activity curtailment plan" to limit the number of extracurricular activities in which any one student could engage,

according to a student handbook at the time:

"The idea is to limit the 'joiners' and the 'socialites' as much as possible and to stimulate shy students. A point system has been worked out, which arbitrarily assigns so many points to each activity engaged in. The maximum points allowed one student being 30."

True to Darwinian Law, some of the organizations that arrived on campus to fill a palpable need twenty, thirty, or seventy years ago, have since departed, replaced by new clubs and associations that meet emerging needs. The hardiest organizations have survived, but even they have evolved over time.

The following pages provide a window into the past and current extracurricular life at Rhodes.

The campus chapter of Habitat for Humanity was the first collegiate chapter to build a Habitat house on its own.

Resident Assistants as a group helped organize this end-of-the-year Twilight Garden Party on the campus lawn during senior week of 1987.

The Literary Societies: "An earnest, jovial set of young men"

The members of Stewart Literary Society in 1900

The Societies' invitation to the 1888 commencement exercises included a portrait of Chancellor Waddel.

From 1852 until 1925, much of the extracurricular life of the school was centered on its two literary societies, the Washington Irving Literary Society and the Stewart Society.

Although they were called literary societies, they were really more on the order of debating clubs, for they met on Friday evenings and, according to a historian of the W.I.L.S. in 1902, "engaged in the delivery of original speeches, the reading of essays, and in debating, conducting the exercises in accordance with strict parliamentary rules."

The W.I.L.S. was formed in 1852 and the following year, "on account of its large membership, some of its members withdrew and organized another society," which was named in honor of the College's new president, William Stewart.

Each society had a clubroom furnished by the school where "an earnest, jovial set of young men met regularly to speak, read, and discuss the questions of the day." Each clubroom had its own library of books supplied by members and friends.

In addition to the debates and speeches within the club, the two

Meeting room of the Washington Irving Literary Society, 1899

societies regularly contended with each other and occasionally with other institutions in public debates and oratorical competitions. In 1909 it was noted that men from the two societies had won seven out of the previous ten statewide competitions of the Tennessee Inter-Collegiate Oratorical Society.

The high point of the year for the societies was the Commencement Contest, when three speakers from each society vied for the Inter-Society Orator's Medal. For many years, it was the societies who issued invitations to the Commencement Exercises.

From 1885 until 1918, the societies joined forces to publish the *Southwestern Presbyterian University Journal*, a monthly magazine of student writing, campus news, alumni news, and college humor. In 1899, they broadened their publishing activities to include the school's first yearbook. Called the *Sou'wester*, it was published sporadically until 1909.

The societies pointed with pride to the number of their alumni whose participation in the clubs' activities had prepared them for successful careers in the

Consumer advocate Ralph Nader takes the Dilemma stage in 1971.

Decades of Debate, Discussion

ministry, law and government. In the early years of the twentieth century, they could boast that two-thirds of the student body belonged to the clubs.

After World War I, however, membership began to decline. The increasing number of other organizations, the growth of the athletic program, the addition of women to the student body, the greater demands on the students' time—all combined to put an end to the Friday night debates. By 1925 both organizations had expired, but they left behind a rich tradition of student self-determination and initiative in the College.

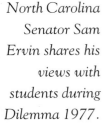

North Carolina Senator Sam Ervin shares his views with students during Dilemma 1977.

Students at the College have never been at a loss for words. Following the demise of the Washington Irving and Stewart Literary Societies, several campus organizations dedicated to discussion and debate arose to take their place. Two of the earliest were the Quibblers and the Nitists. Both groups began in the 1920s: the Quibblers' Forum Debating Club focused on oratory and debate, and the Nitists Club pursued the "discussion of current problems of interest in the world." Abe Fortas '30, who went on to become a U.S. Supreme Court Justice, was a member of both in the late 1920s. William Bowden '48, who later served as president of the College, was president of the Nitists in 1947-48, a year or two before the group faded from the campus scene.

The year 1966 delivered a new avenue for discussing the day's hottest issues: Dilemma—a student-run symposium—was the brainchild of then-student C.V. "Bo" Scarborough '66. It brought to campus well-known speakers for talks and discussions with students. Though its popularity diminished in the late 1980s, until its demise in 1989 Dilemma successfully focused attention on important topics and attracted to campus such major speakers as Ralph Nader, Daniel Ellsberg, Gerald Ford, William Rusher, and Dean Rusk.

Mock Trial, which organized in the late 1980s, follows in the path of other debate-oriented groups on campus. Founded and coached by Professor Mark Pohlmann, the College's Mock Trial teams have, since their establishment, captured the national title four times in intercollegiate mock trial tournaments.

Rhodes' Mock Trial Team, winners of the 1995 national title, pose with their coach, Professor Mark Pohlmann.

The Greeks

Fraternities and Sororities on the Campus and Dates of Establishment:

Fraternities

Pi Kappa Alpha, 1878
Alpha Tau Omega, 1882
Kappa Sigma, 1882
Sigma Alpha Epsilon, 1882
Kappa Alpha, 1887
Sigma Nu, 1934

Sororities

Chi Omega, 1922
Kappa Delta, 1925
Alpha Omicron Pi, 1925
Zeta Tau Alpha, 1929
Delta Delta Delta, 1931
Alpha Kappa Alpha, 1989
Delta Sigma Theta, 1990

Since 1878 fraternities—and subsequently sororities—have been leaving their mark on the College and on the members who join their ranks.

". . . Properly conducted fraternities and sororities are on the whole beneficial to the student."

—President Charles E. Diehl

The original emblem of Pi Kappa Alpha, the first fraternity established at the College

Alpha Tau Omega, 1899

This 1887 photograph of the Kappa Sigma fraternity includes several alumni as well as active members. Note the floral arrangement in the shape of the KS star and crescent.

Pi Kappa Alpha, 1960

Kappa Alpha, 1926

Sigma Alpha Epsilon, 1935

Sigma Nu, 1990

When the College moved from Clarksville to Memphis, the members of the two national sororities and five national fraternities in Clarksville were anxious about the future of their chapters. President Charles Diehl must have eased their worries when he wrote in 1925:

"We believe that properly conducted fraternities and sororities are on the whole beneficial to the student."

He further announced his overall plan for fraternities and sororities:

"The College will assign a piece of ground on the campus for each fraternity or sorority upon which that fraternity or sorority may build a club house of the lodge type, but not a residential house . . . The houses are to be of the same Collegiate Gothic type of architecture, to be constructed of the same material as the other buildings, and are to be harmonious with the whole."

First fraternity to build on the new campus was Kappa Sigma. For the sororities that distinction was held by the Chi Omegas, who moved into a log cabin donated by millionaire entrepreneur Clarence Saunders.

In the 1920s and '30s as much as seventy percent of the student body joined fraternities and sororities. As World

War II heated up, however, membership dwindled. Alumni secretary Goodbar Morgan '31, a Sigma Nu alumnus, described the war's effect on the fraternities:

"As time went on all the fraternities became inactive except SAE and KS. They remained active throughout the four years of the war although their memberships were very small. After the war ended the first regular rush program of any consequence in about four years took place in 1946 . . . With the influx of hundreds of veterans who entered the College under the G.I. Bill of Rights each fraternity pledged large numbers of men—it was not uncommon for most fraternities to pledge anywhere from 24 to 40 men . . ."

From the late 1940s through the mid-'60s, Greek life on campus flourished. During the late 1960s and early 1970s when the Vietnam War, the civil rights movement and student unrest dominated the college scene, fraternities and sororities dipped somewhat in popularity. But in the late 1970s and 1980s they regained stature.

On December 10, 1989, Alpha Kappa Alpha became the first of two historically black sororities to establish a chapter at Rhodes. Delta Sigma Theta colonized at Rhodes the following year. Both sororities are heavily service-oriented.

Today just over half of Rhodes' students pledge a fraternity or sorority. The houses remain non-residential, serving as sites for chapter meetings and social events. The Panhellenic and Interfraternity Councils are the governing organizations of the Greek system. Elected officers and chapter delegates comprise these two governing bodies.

Chi Omega, 1924

Kappa Delta, 1934

Alpha Omicron Pi, 1948

Zeta Tau Alpha, 1952

Delta Delta Delta, 1964

Delta Sigma Theta, 1991

Alpha Kappa Alpha, 1997

The Way They Were:
Greek Houses in 1937

Chi Omega

Alpha Omicron Pi

Kappa Delta

Kappa Sigma

By 1937, five sororities and two fraternities had erected lodges on campus and a third fraternity had completed plans for its proposed lodge. The log cabin housing the Chi Omega chapter was later replaced by a more campus-appropriate stone version. The original wood-frame Zeta Tau Alpha lodge burned in 1946 and was replaced by a stone facility in 1950. That latter facility was reincarnated as the McCoy Theatre after the Zeta Tau Alpha chapter closed its doors in the late 1970s.

The burning issue on campus in April 1956 was the Chi Omega house fire.

House Rules, 1955

This paragraph from the Student Handbook of 1955 outlines the specific rules governing visiting hours at the fraternity and sorority houses:

10. Men and women students are permitted to visit fraternity or sorority houses between the hours of 4:00 and 8:00 p.m. provided that there are always present in the lodge being visited by mixed groups at least eight individuals. When a fraternity house is being visited by women students, there must be present, in addition to at least two junior or senior members of the fraternity, two junior or senior women students or no fewer than four women students from any class. When a sorority house is being visited by men students, there must be present, in addition to at least two junior or senior members of the sorority, two junior or senior men students or not fewer than four men from any class. By noon on Monday, on a form provided for the purpose, fraternities shall submit to the Dean of Men and sororities to the Dean of Women a report on the preceding week stating whether or not the lodge was used by mixed groups under the provisions of this rule.

11. Both fraternity and sorority houses are to be reserved for the exclusive use of men and women respectively during the morning hours and until 4:00 p.m. Monday through Friday and until 1:00 p.m. Saturday.

12. Any unseemly conduct in sorority or fraternity houses or failure to conform to the above regulations will result in disciplinary measures on the part of the Administrative Committee.

House Parties, 1932

Two social events were noted in the February 19, 1932 Sou'wester.

A. O. Pi's Dine In Lodge On Campus

The members of the A. O. Pi Sorority entertained with a banquet last night at 6:30 o'clock in the lodge on the campus. A red and white motif was carried out with a centerpiece of red roses and red and white tapers burning in silver holders. Place cards contained poems for each guest and toasts were made by the President, Virginia Richmond, and Charline Tucker, who presented the ring given each year to the best pledge.

Gals Flock to Levy Fashion show at KD

Levy's Fashion Show drew many of the Southwestern co-eds to the Kappa Delta House Wednesday afternoon, to see the classy chic spring outfits and to hear the soft melodies of Bill Taylor's Collegians, as the boys furnished romance for the co-ed models. Tea and sandwiches were served after the show.

Girls serving as models were: Katy Reid, Margaret Mason, Miriam Heidelberg, Peggy Henderson, Ruth Billings, Dixie Mae Jennings, Julia Marie Schwinn, Peggy Walker, Anita Wadlington, Mary Fay, Mary Anderson, and Sarah Elizabeth Gemmill.

Zeta Tau Alpha

Delta Delta Delta

Sigma Alpha Epsilon

Proposed Kappa Alpha Lodge

Greek Life

Sigma Alpha Epsilon members ride up Main Street in style at the College's annual Homecoming Parade through downtown Memphis.

Kappa Delta members Thelma Nicholas '52 and Ann Brown '50 rustle up laughs during a sorority rush party.

Kappa Alpha fraternity men of the early 1950s deal with the stresses of academic life.

Sigma Nu got into the spirit of Homecoming 1955 with this offering of lawn art depicting a Southwestern rout over Millsaps.

The Chi Omegas welcome a new group of pledges on Bid Day.

Sharing a quiet moment at the Sigma Nu House

Alpha Omicron Pi girls at Stunt Night

Kappa Alpha men enjoy themselves at the 1954 Stunt Night.

All-Sings Considered

The SAE fraternity takes top vocal honors in All-Sing in 1949, the inaugural year.

The AOPi's and ATO's walk off with trophies in the All-Sing competition.

The 1993 Technicolor version of All-Sing has the Kappa Deltas on center stage.

It has been described as "the largest Greek-sponsored social event at Rhodes." In 1948 the College's chapter of Kappa Delta sorority inaugurated All-Sing as a fundraising initiative. KD president Jane Phelps Arnold '49 had witnessed an All-Sing event at Vanderbilt and determined that a similar event would succeed at Southwestern.

Immediately popular, the evening of musical competition attracted enthusiastic participation from the fraternities and sororities on campus. By the early 1960s the groups competing included the Independent Men and Independent Women. Today the range of contestants is as diverse as the roster of organizations on campus.

For the first few years after World War II, proceeds from All-Sing went to sponsor European war orphans. Subsequently Kappa Delta has given the money it raises to the Crippled Children's Hospital in Richmond, one of the KD philanthropies, and to various campus outreach efforts like the student-run soup kitchen at Memphis' St. John's Methodist Church.

Black Student Association

In 1964 the College accepted its first black student, Lorenzo Childress. Five years later, in 1969-70, the Black Student Association was officially organized. "Under the leadership of Julian Bolton the Association has opened up a new era of knowledge and understanding of the Blacks to the college community," read a yearbook description of the nascent organization.

Since then the Black Student Association has been a visible and vital component of the college community, attracting the membership of blacks and whites. Over the years it has hosted a variety of programs, concerts, and exhibits during the year, including the Martin Luther King Birthday Celebration. One of the most popular in recent years has been the Gospel Extravaganza, which hosts gospel choirs from around the region and raises money for a scholarship to Rhodes.

Julian Bolton '71 (inset), who went on from Rhodes to serve as a Shelby County Commissioner, served as the first president of the BSA. In 1969-70, its first official year of operation, the BSA attracted a large and active membership.

BSA events during Black Awareness Week in 1981 included a talent night, a jazz show, and a poetry reading by black authors.

The Renaissance Festival: "Let all hearts rejoice!"

The Great Seal of the Renaissance Festival

Borne aloft by her stalwart courtiers, Good Queen Bess (Professor Betty Ruffin) and her musicians move in procession to open the 1975 Renaissance Festival.

It began as a project of the Drama Department but grew to encompass a number of other departments and organizations—and much of the citizenry of Memphis. Founded in 1974, it continued each spring through 1979, then faltered, resumed again in 1982, and finally faded away in 1985. In its heyday, the Renaissance Festival entertained the college community and townsfolk with excerpts from Shakespeare and other Renaissance playwrights, musical concerts, puppet shows, dancing, craft fairs, jousting and swordplay, poetry readings, alchemy demonstrations, jugglers, and a variety of pageants and processions—all performed outdoors at a number of campus locations.

Craftspeople hawk their wares in the shade of the venerable Rollow Oaks.

Petruchio tames his shrew on the steps of Burrow Library.

The recorder ensemble performs in a variety of costumes, from authentic Renaissance to 1970s hippie style to academic robes.

The flagpole in front of Palmer Hall is transformed into a maypole with frolicking maidens.

Led by Blind Tom, Lady Godiva parades through the campus.

Knights joust on the Back Forty.

Alchemy dazzles the crowd in the amphitheatre.

"In Recognition of . . .": The Honor Societies

President Peyton Rhodes, Professor Robert P. Strickler, and Dr. Gordon White study the charter for the new Gamma Chapter of Phi Beta Kappa at Rhodes.

Phi Beta Kappa inductees pose with faculty and President Rhodes in the Cloister of Palmer Hall.

Omicron Delta Kappa member Frank Boswell '49 taps new member William Hatchett '49 in a ceremony in Hardie Auditorium.

Achievement has rarely gone unnoticed at Rhodes, even in the earliest years. The year 1920 saw the birth of Alpha Theta Phi, which recognized outstanding scholarship, and the Stylus Club—later known as Sigma Upsilon—which saluted top literary ability. Omicron Delta Kappa began life as the Order of the Torch in the early 1920s, evolving into a full-fledged chapter of the national leadership fraternity in 1927.

Since then a host of recognition organizations have sprung to life: Mortar Board, begun in 1964 to salute seniors with stellar records in scholastics, leadership, and service; and a number of honor societies highlighting achievement in the various disciplines of music, physics, classic languages, English, science, history, and others.

At the pinnacle of the College's honor society pyramid, however, rests Phi Beta Kappa, the prestigious national scholastic honorary society. President Diehl began seeking a chapter for the College well before World War II. His dream finally came true December 5, 1949, when the College received the charter for the Gamma Chapter of Tennessee. Rhodes is today one of only 249 colleges and universities in the nation to be awarded a Phi Beta Kappa chapter.

The Honorary Societies at Rhodes

Beta Beta Beta: biology
Eta Sigma Phi: classics
Kappa Delta Epsilon: education
Mortar Board: seniors
Omicron Delta Epsilon: economics
Omicron Delta Kappa: leadership
Phi Alpha Theta: history
Phi Beta Kappa: scholarship
Pi Kappa Lambda: music
Pi Sigma Alpha: political science
Psi Chi: psychology
Sigma Iota Rho: international studies
Sigma Pi Sigma: physics
Sigma Tau Delta: English

Rhodes Organizations: "What's Your Interest?"

Students at Rhodes today can join like-minded students in a rich multiplicity of organizations and communal activities. In addition to thirty varsity, club, and intramural athletic organizations and thirteen social fraternities and sororities, here are some of the other ways Rhodes students get involved.

Student Government
Rhodes Student Government
The Honor Council
The Social Regulations Council
Activities Board
Publications Board

Campus Publications
Cereal Info
Confluence
The Lynx
Rhodes Science Journal
The Sou'wester
The Southwestern Review
The Colossus at Rhodes

Community Service
Campus Green
Habitat for Humanity
Kinney Program
Refugee Assistance
Souper Kitchen

Music
Rhodes College Singers
Rhodes Community Orchestra
Rhodes Mastersingers Chorale
The Wool Socks

Religious Life
Catholic Student Association
Episcopal Student Group
Westminster Fellowship
Fellowship of Christian Athletes
Interfaith Circle
Jewish Student Union
Rhodes Christian Fellowship

Peer Counseling and Support
SHAC (Student Health Awareness
    Committee)
Group

International and Multicultural Activities
All Students Interested in Asia
    (A.S.I.A.)
Amnesty International
Black Student Association
FOSTER*
International House
Model United Nations
Students Talk About Race
    Relations (S.T.A.R.R.)
Women's Forum

Academic Organizations
American Chemical Society
American Marketing Society
Astronomy Club
Film Society
Health Professions Society
Institute of Management
    Accountants
Math/Computer Science Club
Mock Trial Team
Philosophy Club

Greek Life
The Panhellenic Council
    (women's organizations)
Interfraternity Council
    (men's organizations)

Political
College Democrats*
College Republicans*

Administrative Organizations
Admissions Representative
    Organization
Peer Assistants
Resident Assistants

*Rhodes College does not sponsor, endorse, or fund these student organizations.

"If we would understand man, either in society or as an individual, a study of the fine arts is essential."

Campus sculpture by Lon Anthony, 1977

When the College announced an affiliation with the Memphis Academy of Arts in 1947, it did so with these thoughtful words on the role of art in education: "Southwestern believes that no education is completely liberal which has not included at least an elementary study of the fine arts in their traditional and contemporary forms. The profoundest feelings and the essential spirit of an age are always contained, and sometimes exclusively contained, in its artistic record. If we would understand man, either in society or as an individual, a study of the fine arts is essential. The great value of art to civilization makes it obligatory for the student of the liberal arts not only to study the symbols of the past but to help clarify his understanding of today by making his own personal statements. This can only be done by participation in the creative process. By his creative activity in the arts, man realizes and recreates himself and his culture."

Let the Trumpets Sound: Music Comes to the Campus

The Clarksville *Chronicle* of November 18, 1876, reporting on a "grand jollification" to celebrate the election of Democrat Samuel Tilden (the fun was premature, since late results gave the election to Rutherford B. Hayes), noted that among the bands, speeches and fireworks, entertainment was provided by the Glee Club from Stewart College. This is the earliest record of organized musical activity at the school.

Actually, organized may be too strong a word. For the Glee Club and the choirs, bands, string quartets, and guitar and mandolin clubs that formed a part of student life for the next sixty years were not really official college undertakings. Students were encouraged to express themselves musically and to form their own musical groups, but there was no formal instruction in music until the Music Department was formed in 1935. As a result, musical activity swelled or subsided from year to year, depending on student interest and faculty directorial assistance.

The Southwestern Serenaders, 1924

The Guitar and Mandolin Club, 1899

With the arrival of Dr. Burnet Tuthill as director of music in 1935, things changed. Not only did Tuthill institute music classes, he organized a band and a choir, put them firmly in place and nourished them over the years to come. In 1937 he also became director of the well-established Memphis College of Music while continuing his work at the College, and in 1943 he absorbed the College of Music into the Music Department of Southwestern.

As if that were not enough musical activity, Tuthill was made director of the newly formed Memphis Symphony Orchestra in 1938 and conducted rehearsals of that ensemble in the band house (now called Tuthill Hall). A mixture of professional players and students and faculty of the College, the orchestra disbanded in 1947 to be replaced by the all-professional Memphis Sinfonietta.

Today, the Rhodes Department of Music offers a full range of courses both for music majors and for others wishing to enrich their lives with a broader understanding of musical theory and history. The department also offers a series of faculty and student concerts as well as appearances by guest artists. The Rhodes College Community Orchestra—composed of students, faculty and townspeople—presents two or three concerts annually.

The Music Department is also home to the Music Academy of Rhodes College, which offers instruction to more than four

The black and red Russian blouses and berets worn by Dr. Tuthill's first band in 1935 were chosen because they could be made by local seamstresses in ten days' time and be ready for the first football game of the season.

The Galloway mansion (Paisley Hall) at Overton Park Avenue and McLean Boulevard was purchased by the College in 1943 (and renamed Bohlmann Hall after Theodor Bohlmann, founder of the Memphis College of Music) to serve as a home for the Music Department. It was sold in 1970 when the I-40 expressway threatened to roar just outside its back door.

hundred students, from preschoolers to adults, in piano, guitar, and all the symphonic instruments.

The human impulse to make music is one of its happiest ones. The musical program of this College treasures that impulse, cultivates it, and shapes it for the further enjoyment of all.

He Made the College Sing: Burnet Tuthill

His father was the architect of one of the great musical venues of the world, New York's Carnegie Hall. But young Burnet Tuthill did not decide to devote his life to music until he was past forty, when he went to back to school to study composition at the College of Music in Cincinnati. He received his Master of Music degree in 1935 and moved to Memphis that year as director of music at Southwestern.

Burnet Tuthill

Despite his duties running the Music Department, teaching classes, and forming a choir, band and orchestra, he managed to spend his spare minutes composing—music for bands, for choruses, for chamber and symphony orchestras. These pieces were performed by some of the nation's top musical organizations. His "Suite for Band" won the Columbia University Prize in 1947 and was frequently played by the United States Marine Band. "Big River," a musical setting of a poem by John Gould Fletcher, was played by orchestras in New Orleans, Memphis, Oklahoma City, and Jackson, Mississippi. "Bethlehem, Pastorale for Orchestra" was performed by more than fifty orchestras.

But his greatest creation was the love of music he instilled in the hearts of generations of students at the College. They affectionately called him "Papa Tut"—his wife Ruth was "Mama Tut"—and they showed their devotion and respect in every piece they sang for him.

Tuthill consults with Vladimir Golschmann, conductor of the St. Louis Symphony. The Southwestern Singers appeared with the St. Louis Symphony in 1953 and 1954.

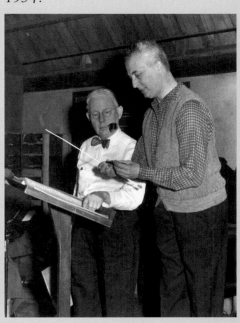

Have Robes, Will Travel: The Singers Become the College's Musical Ambassadors

It did not take very long after Tuthill formed his first choir for the administration to realize that the Southwestern Singers were a valuable promotional asset. This ensemble of personable young people singing beautiful music would provide a very attractive means of introducing the College to a wider community. Accordingly, they supported a tradition that has continued to this day—the spring tour.

The Southwestern Singers prepare to board the bus for a spring tour in the 1950s.

The first tours were brief ones to nearby towns, but as the group became more familiar with the logistics required of a traveling choir, trips became longer and ranged farther afield.

For many years the tour was scheduled over spring break, but now it takes place immediately after graduation, which allows more time for travel. An average tour now lasts ten days, during which the Singers may give as many as fifteen performances. Until recently, most concerts were given in churches, but now a number of daytime appearances in selected high schools are included as well.

Planning a tour usually starts at least eighteen months before the tour dates. A team of student managers works with Professor David Ramsey, accompanist and associate conductor, to select the locations and arrange the schedule.

Among the arrangements that must be made are accommodations for the Singers. In most cities, students are housed in the homes of family-members of the churches where they will sing. Occasionally, the group stays in hotels on weekend nights. Tour managers must also arrange for buses with baggage compartments large enough to carry the Singers' luggage and their voluminous choir robes, which are carefully packed in special containers.

Every third year the Singers replace their usual swing through the southern states with an international tour. Beginning in 1976 with a series of concerts in Romania, they have since toured Poland, Russia, the Czech Republic, Hungary, Scandinavia, and Great Britain.

Wherever they have traveled, the Rhodes Singers have represented the school with spirit, with talent, with taste. They have introduced thousands of listeners to the qualities of genuineness and excellence that Dr. Diehl set down as the College's guiding principles in 1925.

The tour program in 1950 showed the Singers at Bellingrath Gardens, a favorite stop on their schedule.

Discography

The first sound recording of the Singers was made in 1948, under the direction of Dr. Tuthill, of course. Recorded in the music building, the three-disc, 78 rpm album contained selections by Palestrina, Brahms, Randall Thompson, and William Schumann. Since that time, eleven LP recordings and two CDs have been produced. Shown here are the first album and the most recent compact disc, recorded in 1994.

In 1979, the Singers' second European tour took them to Gdansk, Poland.

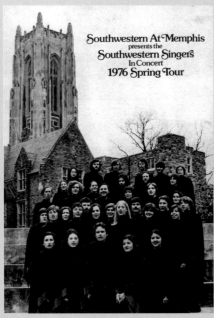

"What if they mutiny?"

Tony Lee Garner '65

When Tony Lee Garner led his first Singers tour in 1967, he was barely out of school himself—and he was terrified. "What if they don't do what I tell them to?" he worried. "What if they mutiny?" After all, only two years before, he had been a Singer himself, and he knew very well just how demanding the students could be of their director. But his musical gifts quickly won him the confidence of the students, and they have sustained his authority ever since. He was director of the Singers for longer than anyone else, including the beloved founder, Professor Tuthill.

Singers shop for souvenirs in Hungary.

Bats, Pals and Players: Theatre at Rhodes

We may never know why the first dramatic organization at this College chose to call itself "The Bats." Was it because the theatre space given to them by the administration was on an upper floor of the Castle? Was it an acronym for Best Acting Theatrical Society?

We do know, however, that The Bats came into being in the spring of 1914 and existed under that name until 1917. During that time they produced short plays in their "portmanteau" theatre, many of which were written by their members and admission to which was issued by invitation only.

We are equally mystified as to why the group changed its name in 1918 to The Pals. (Perhaps because the women who were admitted to the student body in 1917 did not want to be referred to as bats.) As The Pals, productions were expanded to full-length plays, some performed in the larger auditorium of the Clarksville High School. As The Pals, the troupe presented its first production after the move to Memphis—Oscar Wilde's *The Importance of Being Earnest*—in Hardie Auditorium, May 21-26, 1926.

October 1928 brought yet another name change: The Pals became the Southwestern Players. This name stuck for awhile—fifty-four years, in fact, until 1982, when the Theatre Department moved into its new home in the McCoy Theatre and assumed producing responsibilities.

Although Hardie Auditorium was its home base, the Players used every opportunity they could find to produce elsewhere. Designed to be a lecture/assembly/recital hall, Hardie was a far-from-ideal theatrical performance space. So the

The Giant's Stair, *1928*

Everyman *was presented on the north terrace of Palmer Hall, 1937.*

The Importance of Being Earnest, *1974*

Candide, *the first production in the McCoy Theatre, 1982*

Players performed at such downtown theatres as the Lyceum, the Mazda Grotto, and the Ellis Auditorium. They also rented space at the Stable Playhouse and at the Pink Palace home of the Memphis Little Theatre.

Until the hiring of the first full-time teacher of speech and dramatics in 1937, direction of the plays was handled variously by students, faculty, and theatrical enthusiasts from the community.

Under Raymond S. Hill, who took charge of the department in 1949, student involvement increased and the range of the Players' repertory broadened to include more classics and challenging avant-garde works. In 1973, under the direction of Professor Betty Ruffin, the Players carved

out an intimate performing space in the basement of Palmer Hall and called it Theatre Six.

But with the completion of the McCoy Theatre, the College's theatre program finally came into its own. The flexible performance space adapts itself to a wide variety of theatrical forms and production styles. It is this flexibility that enables the McCoy to fulfill its mission: to give the participating students experience with a range of dramatic literature and performance techniques—and to offer the college and community audiences a well-balanced mix of classic and contemporary plays and musicals, intelligently and imaginatively produced.

Richard III, *1997*

Ernest in Love, *1997*

Nicholas Nickleby, 1985. *Student and community actors joined to present this nine-hour epic production.*

Defining the Vision: The Visual Arts at Rhodes

Clough Hall includes studios devoted to painting, sculpture, drawing and life study.

In 1941, having established a Music Department in 1935 and a Speech and Dramatics Department in 1937, Dr. Diehl turned his thoughts to the visual arts. At that time, the only art courses available to Southwestern students were art history courses. Diehl's first step was to hire Robert McKnight, then director of the Memphis Academy of Art, to offer a course at the College in the fundamentals of art.

By 1947, there seemed to be enough interest to support further classes, and a cooperative program was developed with the Academy of Arts through which the Academy (then at 690 Adams Street in the James Lee House) would offer a series of design and painting courses that Southwestern students could take for credit.

Three years later, the Department of Art, under the direction of John Osman, was officially added to the catalogue. The courses were primarily in the history of art, with the continuation of the design and painting courses at the Academy and the addition of a painting class to be taught on campus by a member of the Academy faculty. Finally, in 1955, the first creative art instructor, painter Henry Madden, joined the faculty.

When Madden left in 1961, he was replaced by a young sculptor from South Carolina, Lawrence (Lon) Anthony. Under Anthony's gentle guidance, the Art Department expanded its offerings, brought in the area's leading artists to teach classes, created the College's first gallery exhibition program, and became a vital part of the college community.

As the programs of the Art Department prepare some students for professional careers and some for an enduring appreciation of art, they offer all the opportunity to experience the revelations that art can bring to the human mind and soul.

> ## "I saw the classes I taught in art as a way to knowledge."
> ### —Lon Anthony

Lon Anthony with a work in progress on the deck of his house in the Florida Keys.

For many years he *was* the Art Department of the College, and as it grew, Lon Anthony remained its spiritual center. Not only a wise teacher and caring counselor, he continued to work as a practicing artist, setting for his students an inspiring example of discipline and devotion to work.

In an interview at the time of his early retirement in 1995, Anthony said that he had tried to teach two things. The first was, "Trust thyself. Art is so subjective. Why not trust yourself totally?" And the other thing? "Work. You have to work whether you feel like it or not. If you wait for the muse, you're never going to get anything done."

Anthony also noted that most of his students over the years were not art majors: "I never saw my role as training students to be studio artists. I saw the classes I taught in art as a way to knowledge, another way of understanding yourself, of communicating."

A Window on the World: The Clough-Hanson Gallery

Art can be studied in books and on slides, but there is no true substitute for experiencing it directly—without the intervention of the printed page or slide projector. Providing that direct artistic experience is the mission of the Clough-Hanson Gallery in Clough Hall.

Each year the gallery organizes and mounts a series of exhibitions by faculty and student artists and by outstanding regional artists, introducing the students and the community to a wide variety of artistic expression. National traveling exhibits bring the larger world to the local community. Visiting artists and lecturers add perspective as they discuss the social, political, and cultural issues addressed by various artists.

Just as art can make us look at ourselves and beyond ourselves, the Clough-Hanson Gallery lets Rhodes look at its own artistic world and beyond it.

A Lynx Links Art and Campus

Art major Ann Moore Nunnery '88 brought art and the campus closer together when she took on an assignment in her sophomore year. Professor Lon Anthony asked her if she would be interested in sculpting a figure of a lynx, the school mascot, to be placed on the campus. While a committee deliberated on choosing the site (outside Rhodes Tower above the amphitheatre), she studied the cats at the zoo. After she created several small wax casts of various postures, the committee chose one, and she proceeded to a full-size clay sculpture, then a wax cast, and finally the bronze sculpture. It was unveiled Homecoming Weekend, 1987, a handsome work that joins artistic endeavor with academic achievement.

The Jessie L. Clough Art Memorial for Teaching consists of some two thousand items used for study. Given in 1950 by Miss Floy Hanson, the collection ranges from Japanese prints to textiles and carvings of every description.

LAWRENCE ANTHONY

Diane Hoffman
Paintings 1992–1995
February 27–March 23, 1995
Rhodes College, Clough-Hanson Gallery

Uncouple, 1994, oil on panel

Late nineteenth-century robe belonging to the court of the last Emperor of China

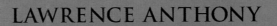

Southern Eye Southern Mind
A PHOTOGRAPHIC INQUIRY

"A great new day for Memphis"

The phrase "town and gown" originated in the Middle Ages, when the great universities were arising in the cities of Europe. The expression implied a certain tension, since frequently the relationship between the university and the town was not an altogether happy one. But conflict has rarely been a part of this college's relationship with the city of Memphis. In 1920, Henry Sweets, Executive Secretary for Christian Education of the Presbyterian Church in the United States, predicted that the establishment of the College in Memphis would be "the coming of a great new day for Memphis." The succeeding years have proven him right: the College has been good for Memphis, and Memphis has been good for the College.

Ten Days in October, 1920:
Memphis Gets a College

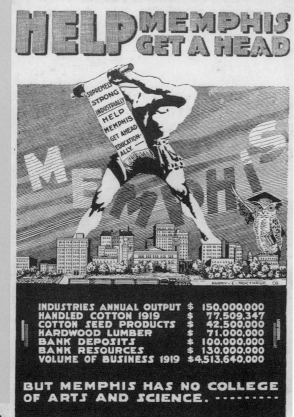

These ads played prominent roles in the "College for Memphis" campaign.

In the years after the first World War, a number of public officials and leading private citizens of Memphis began to express what they felt was a pressing need for this growing, ambitious river town — a liberal arts college. As the only urban area of its size in the country without a college of arts and sciences, the intellectual climate of the city suffered.

At the same time, Southwestern Presbyterian University was feeling constrained in Clarksville. Although it was intended to serve the Synods of Alabama, Mississippi, Tennessee, and Louisiana, the College was located at the extreme northern edge of that large territory. Furthermore, the city of Clarksville had not supplied as many students or as much financial support as had been hoped when the Synods chose Stewart College to be the basis for their new university in 1874. (Memphis had actually been considered for the home of that proposed college, but the recent yellow fever epidemics indicated a somewhat insalubrious air.)

This early sketch of the proposed campus was used in fundraising literature. Obviously, both the layout and the style of architecture underwent radical changes prior to construction. The Jeffersonian domed building at the end of the mall was to be the library. The plan was prepared by distinguished Boston architects Cram & Ferguson, one of the firms Dr. Diehl considered when he was hiring an architect. According to Diehl, the sketch was done mostly for "propaganda"—i.e. promotional purposes.

The city wanted a college, the College wanted a new city: it would seem fated that SPU and Memphis should join hands.

One man well aware of the needs of both the city and the College was Dr. M. E. Melvin, an SPU alumnus and member of its Board of Directors. At the urging of Melvin and prominent businessman E. B. LeMaster, the Memphis Chamber of Commerce took up the cause and offered to mount a campaign to raise $500,000 for the College, contingent upon $1,000,000 being raised from the four Synods. With this backing, Melvin was able to convince his fellow SPU board members that the time was ripe for a move. The decision was approved by the Synods in January of 1920.

In short order, the Chamber of Commerce assembled a committee of outstanding Memphis business and professional leaders, enlisted 350 of its members as fieldworkers, and—with the encouragement of Mayor Rowlett Paine—planned a blitz campaign for October 8-18, 1920. The total raised was $586,000, and on September 16, 1922, construction of the College began.

This was only the beginning of the supportive relationship between the College and the city of Memphis. For a number of years, particularly during the Depression, the College depended upon an annual spring campaign in the city to raise the money needed for operating expenses. Subsequent drives for major funding projects have drawn strong and consistent support from the city, which has well and truly honored its commitment to the College.

Fieldworkers in the ten-day campaign had plenty of sales material to help them. "Spizzerinktum" (a contemporary term meaning vigor or pep) was the title given to the kickoff banquet on October 8 at the Chisca Hotel.

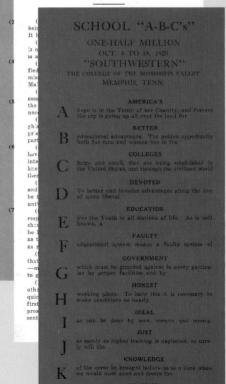

SPIZZERINKTUM

A WORD TO THE WISE IS SUFFICIENT

OCTOBER EIGHTH to EIGHTEENTH
NINETEEN HUNDRED AND TWENTY

The College Honors Its Debt to the City

From its first days, the College was aware of its great obligation to the city. The citizens of Memphis had rallied to the cause and assured the survival of the College by helping it replant itself in more fertile ground.

In exchange, the College offered primarily what the city most desired — a quality education for its sons and daughters. The city responded gratefully: during the '20s and '30s, well over half the students were local residents.

But there was much more to come. From the beginning, members of the college community were encouraged to share their learning with the city at large and to participate fully in church and civic activities.

Dr. Diehl was pleased to note in his annual report to the Trustees in 1932 that Dr. Townsend had presented a series of lectures on Shakespeare to the Nineteenth Century Club, that Dr. Kelso had lectured on medieval and Greek art at Brooks Memorial Art Gallery, and that Dr. A. T. Johnson had addressed the Scribbler's Club of the Junior League on the subject of writing. Such contacts flourished on an ad hoc basis until 1944, when the College formalized the means of sharing its intellectual riches with the citizenry of the town.

In 1944-45, under the auspices of a new program in adult education headed by Professor John Osman, the College offered sixteen evening lectures given by members of the faculty in Hardie Auditorium under the title "The Great Centuries." The audience was largely comprised of members of the community. The success of the series prompted an encore the following year on "Our American Heritage." From these lectures grew a comprehensive Great Books course that has introduced thousands of mid-Southerners to the significant ideas and works of our culture.

In 1954, Professor Granville Davis was

When Burrow Library opened in 1953, it included a meeting room and office space for the Adult Education Center. In 1963, the Center celebrated its tenth year with a party and a cake. Blowing out the candles are Frank Faux, Ray Hill, Granville Davis, Laurence Kinney and May Maury Harding.

The International Cotton Institute

Hosted by Rhodes in association with the American Cotton Shippers Association, the Institute each summer brings to Memphis students from all parts of the globe to learn about one of this region's prime industries. Participants study everything from planting, seed genetics, warehousing and transportation to futures, options, marketing issues, risk management, business ethics and contract law.

The Institute for Executive Learning

For more than forty years, Memphis companies have sent their best and brightest executives to Rhodes to stimulate their interest in the wider world of ideas.

named executive director of the College's Adult Education Center, and with coordinator May Maury Harding introduced a variety of programs designed to help "mature men and women orient themselves to the changing situation of our civilization" and "become fitted for more useful service in business, industry, and church."

The Adult Education Center took seriously its responsibility to the city. Starting in the '50s, in addition to the adult education classes, it initiated a number of projects that brought citizens, officials, and planners together to address such urban concerns as fiscal policy, housing, city planning, transportation, and land use. Many of these projects had direct influence on governmental policies and actions in this city and the region.

Among the most enduring and effective programs has been the Institute for Executive Learning. Initiated in 1955, this innovative course brings middle-management personnel from local businesses together to broaden their perspectives and stretch their minds in reading and discussion of seminal texts.

Another far-reaching project assisted a number of mid-South organizations in developing their planning skills. The Center for Alternative Futures showed businesses, institutions, and civic groups how to set clear goals and determine their own futures.

Although the Adult Education Center became the Meeman Center for Continuing Education, then the Meeman Center for Special Studies, and is now the Meeman Center for Lifelong Learning—and although it has moved its home from the Burrow Library to Clough Hall and finally to Dorothy C. King Hall—it still holds fast to its original purpose: to honor the College's commitment to the city by extending to adult members of the local and business communities the Rhodes tradition of excellence in liberal arts education.

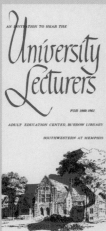

During the 1960s the University Lecturers Series brought outstanding scholars from universities across the country to speak to Memphis citizens.

Rhodes Speaks to the Community

The classes and seminars of the Meeman Center for Lifelong Learning are only part of the Rhodes contribution to the community. A number of lecture series open to the public regularly bring distinguished speakers and performers to share their ideas and talents with the citizens of this area.

Ranging from the visual and performing arts to public affairs to business management techniques to international economics, these prestigious lectures include the Frank M. Gilliland Symposium, the Lillian and Morrie Moss Endowment for the Visual Arts, the Peyton Nalle Rhodes Physics Lecture Series, the M. L. Seidman Memorial Town Hall Lecture Series, and the Springfield Music Lectures.

Thomas J. Peters, co-author of In Search of Excellence, *fires up an audience of mid-South executives in the first C. Whitney Brown Seminar in 1984.*

McCoy Visiting Artists

Agnes de Mille, the celebrated choreographer of Rodeo *and* Oklahoma!, *visited with students after her lecture in 1979.*

Springfield Music Lectures

Renowned composer and conductor Alice Parker, who has collaborated with conductor Robert Shaw on many sacred and choral arrangements, spoke in 1994 about the practice and rewards of choral singing in a joyous lecture-demonstration that was open to the public.

Lillian and Morrie Moss Endowment for the Visual Arts

Robert Hughes, art critic for Time, *and author of* The Shock of the New *and* The Fatal Shore, *was the first Moss Endowment lecturer in 1986.*

Tony-award-winning actress Zoe Caldwell brought Lillian, *her brilliant evocation of playwright Lillian Hellman, to Hardie Auditorium in 1986.*

"... to play the game to the limit of my capacities."
—From the Southwestern Athletic Code, 1925

In a fundraising letter in 1922, Dr. Diehl set forth the College's position on athletics: "Southwestern believes in athletics. Not, indeed, as the main thing in college life, but as an important, a helpful, and a necessary thing. Every man is expected to engage in some sort of physical activity for himself, and not merely to exercise his lungs by yelling from the grandstand."

For Dr. Diehl, the "main thing in college life" was academics, of course, and each succeeding president has reaffirmed the supremacy of brain over brawn. But each has also recognized the value of physical exercise under the stimulus of competition as an important part of the college experience.

Today, twenty-one percent of Rhodes students compete on varsity teams and sixty-five percent participate in intramural and club sports. According to Athletic Director Mike Clary, "It's often said that our athletes play for the fun of it. That's true. But we've found out that it's a lot more fun to win than to lose." And that still means playing the game to the limit of one's capacities.

Let the Games Begin

The Southwestern Presbyterian University football team of 1896

Professor E.M. Mooney, the College's first athletic director

T he College provided its first outlet for the physical energy of its young men in 1871, when the catalogue proudly announced among the College's assets:

GYMNASIUM.

A capital open-air Gymnasium has been recently erected for the use of the students; and due attention will be given to physical health and culture. "Mens sana in corpore sano."

In 1929, Dr. Erskine Brantly, member of the Class of 1873, reminisced in the *Southwestern Alumni Magazine* about that first open-air gym: "The whole field of athletics, with the exception of the trapeze, parallel bars, rings, and perhaps some few other elemental implements used in exercise, was as yet unexplored ground."

By the mid-1880s, organized sports had begun to appear on campus. A Clarksville newspaper reported that on September 6, 1884, "A game of baseball was played on the College campus Wednesday afternoon between a club made up of University students and a town club. The students were entirely too much for the home boys. The game was called in the fifth inning and stood 26 to 7."

Football arrived a few years later. The Clarksville *Tobacco Leaf* of October 1, 1888, noted, "The football made its appearance on the campus last week, at first in the hands of only a few boys but before the afternoon was over about twenty-five enthusiastic fellows were pursuing the ball and good health."

By 1891, the *SPU Journal* could list the official college football and baseball teams, as well as the winners of various track events in the annual field day. With the opening of the new gymnasium in Waddel Hall in 1899 and the hiring of E.M.

The gym in Waddel Hall was described in the 1900 yearbook as "forty feet by sixty feet, the ceiling twenty-two feet above the floor, and having a gallery around its four sides."

Mooney as full-time athletic director, the *Journal* noted that, "He has taken right hold on the work, and has the boys down to it. Much interest is being manifested in basket ball, and it is hoped that a varsity team will be organized." The boys' hopes were soon fulfilled, giving the College four major sports: football, baseball, basketball, and track.

Women were admitted to the College in 1917 and the following year petitioned President Diehl for their own physical education courses; the first women's basketball team took the court in 1919.

Since then the number and diversity of varsity, club, and intramural sports has expanded to include golf, tennis, soccer, softball, volleyball, lacrosse, equitation, and tae kwon do, among others.

Today the varsity teams compete in the NCAA's Division 3, the league for colleges that do not award athletic scholarships. As a founding member of the Southern Collegiate Athletic Conference, Rhodes athletes test their mettle against students from institutions who have an approach to athletics similar to their own.

Clarksville, Tenn.
Nov. 9, 1918

President Chas. E. Diehl,
Southwestern Presbyterian University.

Believing that the purpose of our college training is defeated in part if we do not receive physical as well as mental development, we, the women students of S.P.U., respectfully petition the authorities of the University to provide for us a suitable course in physical education.

Signed: Mary V. Burney
Eleanor Caroland
Essie Sutherland
Chesten Barry
Margaret Trahern
Ursula Smith
Kathrine York
Mildred Taylor
Mildred Smith
Margaret Horwod
Louise Perkins
Margaret Naive (by M.V.B.)

The basketball team of 1899

The 1899 track team

"I Want to Be a Football Hero": Football 1899-1939

It was in the 1920s and 1930s that the athletic hero, particularly the football star, became the icon of school spirit for colleges all across the country. Like knightly champions, these gridiron greats carried the school colors into battle, helped each institution define itself, and gave every student body something to cheer for.

The publicity was also good for the school. Winning teams were powerful public relations tools. After the College moved to Memphis in 1925, the publicity gathered by its successful football teams helped in fundraising and enrollment activities.

From The Pioneer *yearbook, 1925*

This sweater was awarded to Robert Henry Cobb '20 at the first banquet given by the "S" Club, February 19, 1920. This "brilliant affair" was described by *The Sou'wester*: "During the dinner Dabney's Saxophone Orchestra entertained most delightfully with their jazz music and songs. After the dinner Coach Richardson presented the sweaters to the men who had shown the spirit of love for the sport and for love of Southwestern. Each sweater was presented with an appropriate speech, which caused much merriment."

Cobb's sweater was the final one awarded. "Last, and least in size, a sweater was given to the captain of the team of 1919, Cobb, the man of few words, but most successful and proficient in action, and the one who made the wonderful end-runs which often brought victory to the 'Red and Black.'"

The sweaters for the athletes were purchased with funds raised by an entertainment presented under the auspices of The Pals dramatic club. In announcing plans for the event, *The Sou'wester* noted: "There will be a large cast, mixed, the ladies possibly wearing full dress suits, while the men will appear in feminine attire, appropriate for formal evening dress."

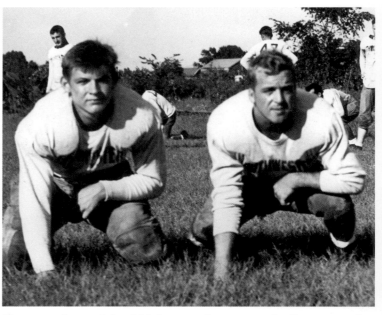

Two members of the 1936 team, known as the "iron men," Guard Richard Parker and Captain "Toto" Houts.

Southwestern vs. Ole Miss, sometime in the 1930s. Helmets seem to have been optional equipment. Did they have harder heads or softer linemen back then?

These program covers for Lynx games in the 1930s were created by nationally known sports artist Lon Keller, who also designed the logos for the New York Yankees and the New York Mets.

SOUTHWESTERN vs. TENNESSEE

OFFICIAL PROGRAM
PRICE 25¢

NOVEMBER 9, 1940 • CRUMP STADIUM • MEMPHIS

LYNX VS. OLE MISS

OCTOBER 7, 1939
PRICE 25 CENTS

OFFICIAL PROGRAM

PRICE 25¢

SOUTHWESTERN vs. CENTENARY

This page from the 1939 yearbook tells the story: it was a very good year.

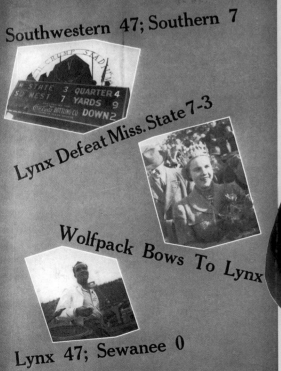

Southwestern 47; Southern 7

Lynx Defeat Miss. State 7-3

Wolfpack Bows To Lynx

Lynx 47; Sewanee 0

Dr. Diehl wore this green hat to football games for twenty years. In 1951 it became the prize passed on each year to the winners of the Alumni Day softball game.

A College Game, Not a College Business: Football 1940-98

Home games in the 1930s were frequently played at Crump Stadium to crowds of 10,000 or more. Tickets shown are for the five home games played there in 1941.

The Edmund Orgill Bowl is engraved with the results of the football games between Rhodes and the University of the South at Sewanee since 1954. The winner of the annual game between the two holds the bowl until the next game. At the end of the 1997-98 season, the score is tied, with twenty-two victories for each school.

In December of 1940, after several highly successful football seasons, Southwestern startled the community by announcing that it would no longer subsidize athletes with free room and board. By this action, the Executive Committee of the Board of Directors said, the College hoped to become "one of the leaders in a group concerned with preserving football as a college game and not as a college business."

The Sou'wester editorialized against the position, predicting that it would mean the end of collegiate football for the school. "If a team had to be chosen from the male students on campus, outside of those receiving athletic scholarships, we would not have anything to compare with the average Memphis high school."

But Walter Stewart, sportswriter for *The Commercial Appeal*, approved the decision. "This follows a rising sports trend in which the smaller schools sheer away from the big leagues. This is largely as it should be . . . a squad of twenty men has no business matching beef with five-team hordes which can produce it by the solid ton."

Still, it was a risky position to take. In 1936, *The Commercial Appeal* had reported on a luncheon held by 200 leading business and civic leaders to congratulate the football team on their 12-0 victory over Vanderbilt and on the national attention they were bringing to Memphis. By taking Southwestern out of "big time" football, the College might lose some much-needed financial support. But the Executive Committee held fast to its principles, and still support for the program continued.

Today Rhodes students who receive financial aid based on need or merit may indeed include athletes. But they earn their scholarships with their brains, not their brawn. And the College's athletic program remains the way it was originally envisioned, an important adjunct to a liberal education. "*Mens sana in corpore sano.*"

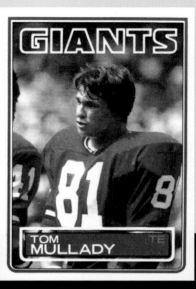

Tom Mullady '78 was such an outstanding player that his number was retired. He joined the Giants in 1979, and in 1982 his twenty-seven catches led Giant receivers.

The 1971 team rang the bell as co-champions of the College Athletic Conference

Mike Lee '96 (with ball) established a new single-season rushing record in 1995 by rushing for 1,392 yards en route to leading the Lynx to the SCAC title.

Football was suspended during the World War II years 1942-45. Play resumed in 1946, but it took a few years for the struggling team to get on its feet. Then in 1951, during the Korean War, football was suspended again, to be restored in 1952 under a new coach, Glenn A. Johnson. Although the team won only one game in 1953, the players were so overjoyed they lifted Coach Johnson to their shoulders.

The Nineteen-Year Time-Out:
Lynx Baseball

From The Pioneer *yearbook, 1925*

Baseball, one of the College's original sports, was very popular in the early years of the century. According to an athletic history written in the 1920s, "For several years, SPU had a baseball team which ranked with the very best in the South. Sewanee, Vanderbilt, U. of Ala. and others lost to our team." The anonymous historian goes on to note several SPU players who went on to play major-league ball, then tells of a memorable series in 1917 when SPU defeated Vanderbilt: "On the team's return to the city our president gave the team enough money to see several shows, drink all the sodas they wanted, and to have a good time in general."

After the move to Memphis, however, and the increasing dominance of football, interest in baseball waned; in 1930 it was dropped as a varsity sport. The College's precarious financial position due to the Depression undoubtedly played a part in this decision.

When baseball returned to the varsity lineup in 1949, the yearbook referred to it as "a sport brand new to Southwestern."

Since then this old/new sport has continued as an important part of the athletic picture at the College.

The 1908 baseball team—a dapper bunch indeed.

In 1961 the team took a first in the NCAA College Division Mideast Region.

Steve Johnson lets one fly, 1970.

On April 18, 1989, the Lynx played an exhibition game against a team from the USSR who were touring the country to get baseball experience and to learn from American teams. Rhodes won 12-6.

1995: looks like a good one.

Basketball: The Original Equal Opportunity Sport

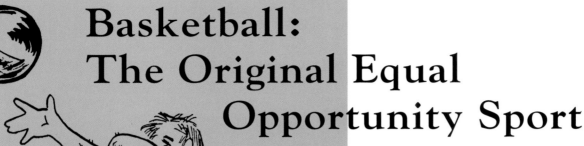

From the 1927 yearbook

The stairstep men of 1924, the last team from Clarksville.

The men basketball players were ready, willing, and able to go when the first gym was built in 1899; they had a team on the floor before the season was out. Similarly, when women were admitted to the College in 1917, they lost little time in getting their act together; as their picture shows, the first team was ready for action in 1919.

The men's teams were soon playing a schedule of opponents from nearby colleges. The 1909 schedule, for example, included Vanderbilt, Cumberland University, and the University of Nashville.

It was a little more difficult for the women to put together a schedule. They had no coach, no place to practice, and they were not permitted by the College to take overnight trips out of town. But they persisted, and by 1927 they were being coached by two players from the men's varsity team and had been granted access to the new gym in Fargason Field House three days a week. Their opponents were teams from Memphis high schools and the YWCA.

The 1927 yearbook gave equal space to the two basketball teams.

The carefully coiffed women's team of 1919.

Men's Basketball:
Through Good Years and Bad

After fielding several promising teams in the 1920s and '30s, the men's basketball program hit the doldrums in the '40s and '50s before rebounding in the '60s. Today's teams are again winning conference championships and playing in national tournaments.

Even though football was discontinued during the World War II years, the basketball program kept on rolling. Is this picture of the 1945 team an ironic comment on their lack of tall players?

The team of 1951-52 had a lot to overcome. The previous year had seen a fifteen-game losing streak, a players' strike due to unhappiness with the coaching, the disbanding of the team mid-season, and the resignation of the coach. Here, with a new coach, the survivors get ready for a game.

The 1969 team came out on top in the Dixie Tournament.

1981. Chitwood gets a boost from the opposition.

Kittens on the Court

From The Lynx *yearbook, 1927*

Started while the College was still in Clarksville, women's basketball was elevated to varsity status after the move to Memphis in 1925. For the next five years, the Kittens (as they were called) played a limited schedule with local and nearby teams. But in 1931 the yearbook announced that because "there were not enough women in the school who could devote enough time to practice sessions, it was found necessary to discontinue the usual collegiate basketball team."

For the next forty-two years, when women's athletics were confined to a range of intramural sports activities, class and sorority basketball teams were organized

This Squad of Husky Kittens Will Uphold Black and Red

The Kittens of 1927 may not have been too happy with the headline writer's adjective for them.

The women's team of 1984 added this championship trophy to the display cases in the Mallory-Hyde lobby.

1989: Libby McCann heads for a better shooting position.

into a league with trophies for the winners. Starting near the end of the 1930s, college teams were sometimes formed from the top players in the intramural league and games were scheduled with some local high-school and other college teams.

A varsity team was finally re-established in 1972, but it didn't stick. It was not until 1975 that women's basketball was firmly in place as a part of the varsity program. Since then it has flourished and developed into one of the strongest elements in the Rhodes athletics program.

Soccer Kicks onto Campus

The men's soccer team won the NCAA Division III championship in 1996 and participated in the NCAA Division III National Playoffs in 1994, 1995, and 1997.

Soccer materialized on the Rhodes campus in the 1960s as a sort of counterculture sport. Taylor Phillips '79 remembers soccer games at the College in 1975: "We played at Overton Park against local clubs, on a field with no nets on the goals, no corner flags, and more mud and potholes than grass. The two or three women played on the men's team. With the odd assortment of beards, bandannas, earrings, ponytails, boxer shorts hanging out, and ROTC boots, we looked more like some expedition lost in a jungle than a team."

By the fall of 1976 the men had a coach, red uniforms, a collegiate schedule, and permission to play home games on the football field. And the College had a new varsity sport.

Within a couple of years, enough women had become interested to form a club team (with Taylor Phillips as their coach) and in 1983 women's soccer was officially given varsity status. Since then both teams have consistently brought honors to the College with Division and Tournament championships. Both teams have also represented the College abroad, traveling to Europe to vie with teams over there.

Lynx player Tripp Dargie goes head to head with the competition in this 1984 game

The women's soccer team took top honors in the Rhodes College Invitational Soccer Tournament in 1993.

At the net, 1994

Track and Cross-Country at Rhodes

The winged feet of the College's team brought victory in the 1957 Memphis Relays.

It was mankind's first competitive sport—to determine who could run the fastest, throw the longest, jump the farthest or highest. Track was the College's first organized athletic activity, too. Field days featuring track events were held on the campus in the late 1880s, and in 1899 the College's first yearbook pictures a track team.

After an off-and-on series of seasons in the 1920s, track subsided to an intramural sport but was restored to varsity status in 1929. The track teams of the 1930s performed well and gave the College a good reputation in field events. After World War II, cross-country competition was added to the varsity roster and quickly became another major prizewinner. The men's cross-country team has won eight consecutive Southern Collegiate Athletic Conference championships; the men's track and field team has won five SCAC championships since 1990.

The 1931-32 track team placed first in the Dixie Conference and third in the Southern Intercollegiate Athletic Association.

Women's track and cross-country emerged as varsity sports in 1978 and now hold their own with their brothers. The women's track and field team won conference championships in 1995 and 1996; the women's cross-country team has won three consecutive championships.

The 1964 cross-country team had the eighth winning season in a row for the College.

Hurdling in the 1980s

Running cross-country, 1990s

Sprinting in the 1970s: Herman Morris, Levi Frazier, Todd Robbins, Jeff Carter

Leading the way to the tape, 1994

Seeds of Distinction: Tennis at Rhodes

The gentlemen of the 1900 tennis club sit for their portrait in a stylish array of headgear.

The tennis club seems to have been a permanent fixture on the college campus from the 1890s on, but it was not until the mid-1920s that an official team began playing scheduled matches with other institutions.

Women's tennis remained at the intramural level until March of 1972, when a varsity team was formed and promptly won its first match against Lambuth 7-2.

In 1997, the men's team was ranked in the top thirty-five in the nation and the top thirteen in the South. The women's team ranked fifteenth (out of three hundred) in the nation and fifth in the South.

Two of the three members of the College's 1925 tennis team

The 1940 tennis team had a very successful season, winning nine out of eleven matches. Their proud coach was physics professor Peyton N. Rhodes, later President of the College.

Derrick Barton, tennis coach in the 1950s (back row, left), produced a series of winning teams and top-flight players. Among the latter was Tommy Buford '57 (front row, second from left), recently named to the Rhodes Athletic Hall of Fame.

One of the finest players ever to grace the Rhodes courts, Nao Kinoshita '98 won the 1995 and 1997 NCAA Division III National Singles Titles. With her partner, Taylor Tarver '98, she also won the 1997 NCAA Division III Doubles Title.

Athletics for Everybody:
Intramurals at Rhodes

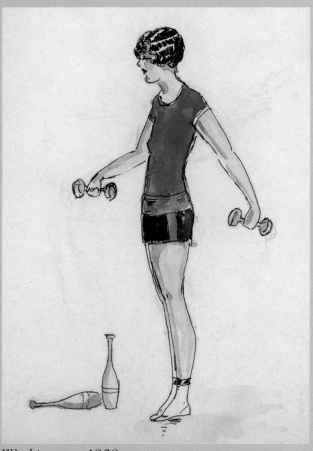

Working out, 1928

Horseshoes in the 1930s

Intramural (literally, "within the walls") athletics traditionally involve teams from the same institution. But at Rhodes that definition is far too narrow. From their beginning, intramural activities at the College have encompassed individual competition as well as team sports.

Intramurals are open to everyone, not just the skilled athlete; they're for students who lack the time or facility for varsity sports, yet wish to exercise their bodies, test their skills, and just have fun with students of similar abilities. As one would expect, there are more of these part-time athletes than there are varsity players.

Intramurals have included everything from ping-pong and fencing to racquetball and walleyball, according to the taste of the times and the interest of the students. After all, intramurals offer something for everyone.

Shooting in the 1930s

Archery and ballet in 1946

Softball in the 1950s

From 1930 until 1972, the only athletics for women were the intramural ones. The range of these sports is shown in this photograph from the 1957 yearbook. Other activities that year were fencing, archery, ping-pong and modern dance.

Flag football—or "flagball," in campus vernacular—in the 1970s

V-I-C-T-O-R-Y:
Leading the College Cheers

College Yells
The following are the College yells:

FIRST
With a vevo! with a vivo!
With a vevo vivo vum vum!
Johnny get a rat trap bigger than a cat trap
Johnny get a cat trap bigger than a rat trap
Hannibal! Hannibal! sis boom bah!
Varsity! Varsity! Rah! Rah! Rah!

SECOND
S. P. U. rah! rah!
S. P. U. rah! rah!
Hoorah! Hoorah!
Varsity! Varsity! Rah! Rah! Rah!

THIRD
Rackety kax! ko-ax! ko-ax!
Terreorex-o-rex-orex!
Hulla-baloo! Hulla-baloo!
S. P. U.

FOURTH
S. P. U. is our cry
V-I-C-T-O-R-Y!

The Student Handbook of 1915 prescribed these yells for freshmen to learn before the first game of the season.

Vocal support seems to be essential to major crowd-pulling sports. How can you truly enjoy a fast-moving football or basketball game without the opportunity to show your support or disapproval by shouting at will and occasionally chanting in unison?

If we go by the published yells, cheers were more complex in the early days than they are today. But they didn't have the dance and pompom routines that inspire and ignite today's crowds.

1930: no fancy costumes, no elaborate routines, just a few guys with loud voices and a megaphone.

Collapsible megaphones such as this one helped the crowds cheer louder in the 1930s. They were supplied to fans by the Kroger Company.

Classic Americana, 1958: white letter-sweaters, circle skirts, radiant faces.

1984: short skirts, snappy steps, same spirit and enthusiasm.

1969: pompoms enter the picture.

The Haygood Athletic Hall of Fame

Gaylon Wesley Smith '39

In 1937, running back Gaylon Smith from Beebe, Arkansas, spearheaded the Lynx to their most successful season since 1896. He led the entire nation in scoring for two weeks, finally coming in third in the country with ninety-seven points for the season. In basketball he played forward and was the leading scorer for three consecutive years. A four-year letterman in track, Smith set pole-vault and hundred-yard-dash records that were to stand for many years.

Henry Thomas Hammond '36

Native Memphian "Ug" Hammond was a member of the legendary 1936 Lynx football squad that lives in history as the twelve "iron men." In this one season he scored against Union University, twice against Millsaps, once against Birmingham-Southern and Loyola University. But it was the Vanderbilt game that climaxed his career: he caught a pass for the final touchdown and a 12-0 win over the highly touted Nashville team. Newspapers throughout the South reported it as "no miracle, but a well-deserved triumph."

Ralph Clinton Allen '73

The *Memphis Press-Scimitar* said it best: "There probably isn't a college athlete in this land with more versatility than Southwestern's Ralph Allen." In football, he was named to the All College Athletic Conference team. In basketball, his coach called him "our best hustler and best defensive man." In track he was a virtual one-man team, setting college records that still stand in the decathlon and javelin. In 1972 he qualified for the NCAA College Decathlon and was named All American, the school's first track-and-field athlete to earn this distinction.

In 1996, the College inaugurated its Athletic Hall of Fame, honoring the outstanding athletes of its past and preserving their memory for future generations. The Hall of Fame is located in the Bryan Campus Life Center and is named in honor of James "Jimmy" Haygood, who served the College as athletic director and head football coach in the 1930s. Each year nominations to the Hall of Fame are solicited from the Rhodes community and new names are added to the roster. The first six honorees are shown here.

Freeman Carl Marr '48

As student track standout, alumni association president, and volunteer coach, Freeman Marr has never stopped running for his alma mater. In 1947 he ran on the Lynx mile relay team that set a state collegiate record. During his senior year, Marr set a national collegiate record in the pentathlon. From 1956 to 1967 he returned to the campus to serve as men's track coach on a volunteer basis, coaching teams that won an outstanding fifty-two meets. In 1978 he started Southwestern at Memphis's first women's track team, known at the time as "SAM's Angels."

Thomas Bright Buford, Jr. '57

He came to Southwestern to play baseball but was soon recruited to the tennis team by coach Derrick Barton. He

rewarded his coach's confidence by winning the Tennessee Intercollegiate Championship in 1956 and 1957. Buford became head tennis coach for the University of Memphis in 1966 and since then his Tigers have scored 412 wins versus 235 losses and have won five conference championships. As tournament director of the Kroger St. Jude Classic at the Racquet Club he has been voted by tour professional players as one of the top six tennis officials in the world.

Southwestern's Athletic Code

As an athlete I am determined—

1. To play the game to the limit of my capacities, giving each detail the greatest care and attention.

2. To strive to carry more than my own burden, to do a little more than my share, not seeking help from others.

3. To correct my faults, ever eager to learn and improve, never seeking to cover up or conceal mistakes made.

4. To carry the fight to the opponents with the spirit of the "Old Guard" that dies but never surrenders.

5. To be unselfish in endeavor, caring more for the satisfaction which comes from doing a thing well than for praise.

6. To glory in fighting against odds like the Lacledæmonians, who never asked of the enemy "how many are there?" but "where are they?"

7. To hate an alibi, knowing that the man who makes excuses admits his weakness and has a dwarfed soul.

8. To rise above obstacles, to fight harder when the game is going the other way than when winning.

9. To fight with an unconquerable spirit, realizing with every act that "the deed is the measure of the man."

10. To play according to the letter and the spirit of the rules, scorning an unfair advantage over an opponent.

11. To remember that the measure of achievement is not the victories won, but how I played the game.

12. To be undismayed by defeat, but with a will hardened by adversity seek to learn the cause of failure.

13. To be unspoiled by victories, realizing that brave men are softened by success rather than by defeat.

14. To give the best that is in me, to the end that I may be a better student, a better citizen, a better man.

Southwestern's Athletic Code

In the mid-1920s the College published the above code for its athletes to play by. Although the language may seem archaic and occasionally stuffy to us today, the ideas embodied in the code are in no way foreign to the rules of fair play, honesty, and self-discipline that drive Rhodes athletes at the end of the century.

Harold Walter "Chicken" High '33

A legend in the annals of Lynx athletics, Harold "Chicken" High was called by a sportswriter of the 1930s "one of the greatest ball toters in Dixieland." High excelled in basketball, track, and football (he captained the 1932 Lynx football squad) and was named quarterback on the all-star Southern Intercollegiate Athletic Association team. In 1933 he joined the athletic staff as assistant football coach, freshman basketball coach, and varsity track coach. He continued as a key member of the athletic staff until he resigned to enlist as a lieutenant in the United States Army.

The Orientation Team tries to answer freshmen's questions about life at Rhodes. Considering the multiplicity of activities here, it's not an easy job.

"A good mix between the worthless and the worthwhile."

—The Student Handbook, 1974

Chapter Eleven: Student Life

The Student Handbook for 1974 prepared incoming students with these words, "Social life is what one makes it . . . by nature it is informal and spontaneous . . . a good mix between the worthless and the worthwhile."

Actually, that's not a bad prescription for social life anywhere, since even the most serious and responsible life needs its lighter moments. At Rhodes, students have found relaxation in a dizzying variety of ways—some are worthwhile, some are worthless, but all are important in preparing for life in the larger world.

The Men's Residence Halls

SOPHOMORE CLASS

Sophomores and Seniors

Drawings from the 1908 yearbook contrast the lifestyles of sophomores and seniors.

SENIOR CLASS

"Nothing is more demoralizing."

"It is notorious that nothing is more demoralizing, even in the case of mature men, than that they gather in crowds in any capacity habitually, in clubs, from which are excluded the more elevated class of females. This is found to be more universally the case among boys and young men. This danger is greatly aggravated by their being congregated together in adjacent sleeping chambers at night. Instead of spending their time in application to study, which is the prime object in view in this system, they are tempted to visit each other, to play at unlawful games, or to go out, under cover of the darkness of night, to places utterly ruinous to health and morals."

—Chancellor Waddel (1879-88) on the housing of students in dormitories

VICS ARE TABOO IN BOYS' ROOMS

College Lays Down Law Regarding Music

College officials are very emphatic in their announcement that students are not to have victrolas in their rooms. The only victrolas to be played on the campus are those in the social rooms.

No musical instrument of any kind will be played before 1 p. m. and after 7:30 p. m. Students desiring to play any instrument besides the victrola may do so in their rooms in the afternoons only.

Student dormitory leaders as well as resident faculty members in each will see that these rules are enforced. New dormitory leaders are L. P. "Doc" Watkins, Robb Hall; T. M. Garrott, Calvin Hall; and Crawford McGivaren, Stewart Hall. Faculty members in the dormitories are Prof. W. R. Cooper, Robb; Prof. J. A. Ross, Jr., Calvin, and Prof. R. F. Thomason, Stewart.

—*The Sou'wester*, September, 1927

The Dormitory as a Benefit to Moral Nature

The humorous side of life is capable of being largely added to in a dormitory. It is a very happy faculty to be able to see the amusing side in the happenings of life, and fortunate is the man who does not take himself too seriously. The midnight feasts and jokes, and the carousals in the early morning hours in which you are a listener and not always a participant, go to great lengths in developing a humorous nature and a pleasure in the pursuits of others. The fact that we may laugh at the expense of others and hear others laugh at us is like a tonic in bringing our moral natures to a higher pitch of bigness."

—Editorial, *SPU Journal*, February 1915

The '20s

'30s Study Group

Calvin Hall, 1:15 a.m. Tuesday

Sleeping like two little birds in a nest,
C.C. and Wharton are sweetly at rest.
Wardlaw and Jocco are also asleep—
Through the cracked window the round moon doth peep.
Bachman and Hooper have just gone to bed—
Hooper is tired and says he's 'most dead.
Jacob is sleeping alone, don't you know?
He has no roommate, because he snores so.
Vip's in his chronic state, happy at rest,
Lying asleep and a'rolling his best.
Davis retired at about half-past ten,
He's sleeping real soundly like all gentlemen.
Raymond and Egg have no trouble to snooze,
They're both feeling happy, they're both full of booze.

—*SPU Journal*, May 1914

'50s Study Group

'90s Study Group

The Women's Residence Halls

The Iron Curtain

In the '40s and '50s no man was allowed beyond this velvet barrier in Voorhies. Nearby were the nooks called "passion pits" where torrid goodbyes were made.

OUT

NAME MARTHA HEINEMANN

CLASS JUNIOR   ROOM NUMBER 110

DATE	LEAVE HOUR	DESTINATION AND COMPANION	RETURN HOUR
2-24	9:15	out to eat	9:40
2-26	6:00	lecture	9:00
2-27	8:00	Death of a Salesman	10:55
3-2	6:55	ball game	8:20
3-3	6:45	ball game	8:20
3-7	7:00	show	10:00
3-12	7:00	ball game & lab	10:10
3-19	6:00	Chi Beta Phi banquet	8:00
3-21	6:30	Stunt Night	10:55
3-23	8:00	movie - AEC	9:50
3-23	9:55	out to eat	10:30
3-31	7:30	movie	11:00
4-2	8:30	biology lab	9:45
4-8	7:50	"Dear flow"	11:15
4-10	8:50	out to eat	9:30
4-11	9:45	show	12:45
4-12	7:20	out to eat	8:00
4-24	6:30	AEC to movie	9:10
4-25	7:30	"Lear"	12:50
4-27	8:10	drug store	8:30
4-30	8:45	Parkside	9:30
5-2	7:45	show	11:00
5-3	7:45	Evergreen	9:15
5-5	6:05	biology lab	9:55
5-6	7pm	Opera	11:40
5-7	7pm	opera	11:45
5-10	7:45	out to eat	8:25
5-13	7:00	cotton carnival	9:05
5-13	9:50	eat	10:25
5-15	9:10	out to eat	9:45
5-16	9:30	movie	12:30
5-18	9:30	eat	9:55
5-19	5:35	biol. lab	10:50
5-21	10:10	eat	10:40
5-22	10:00	"	10:40
5-23	10:20	out to eat	11:20
5-25	9:20	Toddle House	9:35
5-27	7:30	miniature golf	8:35
6-1	8:30	out to eat	9:00

Evergreen Hall

The first residence hall for women was Evergreen Hall, a converted apartment building on University, across the street from the main campus.

Where in the World Was Martha Heinemann?

Junior Martha Heinemann's sign-out card for the spring of 1959 records when she left Voorhies for trips to the Metropolitan Opera, the Memphis Shakespeare Festival, the biology lab, and the Toddle House.

Dr. Diehl Recommends a Clarksville Women's Dormitory

"The girls who attend here from out of town board with Mrs. Frank Beaumont, who is an estimable, refined, Christian woman. The dormitory is beautifully located, is accessible to the College, and Mrs. Beaumont looks after the girls with personal solicitude. She is a very unusual woman. She takes the girls at a reasonable rate, about $5 or $6 a week, and I think that you can arrange with her for your daughter. Some of our girls were there last year and found it very pleasant."

—Dr. Diehl, in a letter to a parent, 1923

Snacking in the '50s

The Voorhies Salon

Before the days of portable hair dryers, the women's residence halls provided basement rooms equipped like mini-salons.

Living in the '90s

Feeding the Student Body

Complaining about food has been a favorite student pastime since the Middle Ages. Generations of cooks, nutritionists, and dietitians have struggled mightily to please the student palate with, as one might expect, varying degrees of success. Imagine 1,400 people, from just as many households, eating in the same dining hall. Now imagine them agreeing on the food.

Food Joke, 1913

Shepard: "I left a mark that will endure for ages, I cut my name on one of the rocks in Dunbar's Cave."

Hill: "Mine will endure far longer; I scratched mine on a piece of Robb Hall pie crust."

—*SPU Journal*, February 1913

College Comment

To Our Cook, Harrison

Hail to thee, blithe Harrison!
Cook thou always wert,
Or if not a cook, so near it
That we haven't heart
To disparage thine unpremediated
     art.

Harder boiled, still harder,
Every day thou seem'st to be;
Would'st thou eat from thine own
     larder
The pudding that thou feedest me?

Oh, those golden eggs so stenching,
Golden like the sun;
Eggs from which hog grease is
     drenching,
Eggs which float and run,
Like an unbodied joy whose race is
     just begun.

Lean also is thy bacon on thy bill
     of fare,
We take it every other morning,
We take it leisurely with care.
'Tis so small it soon has vanished,
Yet we know that it was there.

Pills we take "before and after,
And we pine for what is not; •
Our sincerest laughter
With inner pains is fraught,
Our sweetest sons tell of eats from
Kuhn's that we have bought.

Yet couldst thou teach me half the
     mixtures
That thy brain must know—
Ah! my dear, dear Harrison,
From my hands would flow
Grub so all the world might eat—
     as I am eating now.

Food Poem, 1926

—*The Sou'wester*, May 21, 1926

After the Catherine Burrow Refectory had acquired the affectionate nickname "the Rat"—short for "Rat Factory"—student sculptor Allen Bell created this stone realization of it, which now graces the entrance walkway.

A Few Words from the Chef

—*The Commercial Appeal*, November 6, 1936

College Students Favor Vegetables, Leon Powers, Veteran School Chef, Says

Young Folks Who Several Years Ago Wanted Only Steak and Potatoes Now Go in For Variety

BY TOMMY FULLER

Young people have shown a decided "vegetable trend" during recent years, Leon Powers, veteran chef of the Southwestern kitchen, believes. Mr. Powers, known to the kitchen crew and students as "captain," has been cooking young people's food for 15 years and says he "wouldn't quit it for anything."

Becoming college chef in 1921, when Southwestern was located at Clarksville, Mr. Powers says he can remember when students weren't satisfied with anything but steak and potatoes, but now "a good meal including snap beans, buttered carrots, scalloped potatoes, corn muffins and a mixed fruit salad with marshmallows would fill the bill."

"We even get calls for spinach, beets and squash, when 10 years ago we wouldn't expect such vegetables to be eaten. Yes, sir, college tastes as well as the quality of food has changed," he said.

And contrasting the food of today with that of a generation ago, "Captain" Powers pointed that more salads and "dressed" meals were served in colleges now than in fancy restaurants of the past.

"However, the old standby of broiled steak, French fried potatoes, green peas, hot rolls, preserves and apple pie a la mode isn't turned down, even by the young freshman fresh from 'mama's good cooking.'" "Captain" calls this his steak special and had rather prepare it than anything else.

When asked to name the favorite college menu for a day, he said:

"The breakfast is composed of fruit or orange juice, cereal, flannel cakes and coffee.

"The noon meal of broiled onions, snap beans, escalloped potatoes, muffins, fruit salad.

"Dinner is either broiled steak or filet mignon, French fried potatoes, green peas, rolls and apple pie, as against fried chicken, giblet gravy, steamed rice, buttered asparagus and angel food cake with ice cream."

During the 26 years he has been in the cooking business, Mr. Powers has picked up quite a few "tricks of the trade." The best way to prepare fresh peas is to cook them with as little water as possible, with the top off the boiler to preserve the green freshness, he said. "The cauliflower au gratin may be prepared best by boiling in salt water in an open kettle for about 20 minutes, and then adding a rich cream sauce with cheese," he added.

"Captain's" first job was in 1905 as waiter in a Clarksville restaurant, where he stayed until 1910, when he went to cooking for a "short order house." From there he took a position with the Colonial Hotel at Springfield, Tenn., where he stayed until taking his present job with the college.

During summer vacations, Mr. Powers usually works in boys' camps, where he can keep in contact with the "young folks," which is the best thing about his job, he says. For seven years he cooked in a boys' camp at Brevard, N. C., of which George Morris, assistant

Eating in the '80s

In 1987, *Sou'wester* editor Luke Lampton, in a three-column diatribe against the management of the refectory, sounded a contemporary health-conscious note:

"They need to redirect their energies toward providing a more healthy, delectable and satisfying diet for Rat diners ... I seriously question the effects that these starchy, greasy, cholesterol-permeated meals have on our health. For someone on the board plan, there is no grease-free alternative short of eating salads or Cheerios at every meal, which quickly becomes old."

Noshing in the '90s

Diners in today's refectory have choices to satisfy a wide variety of appetites and inclinations.

Servery A provides traditional hot meals with meat and meatless entrees, vegetables, burgers, and the like. A multi-choice salad bar also includes dress-your-own baked potatoes. There is also a dessert bar, a bagel bar, a fruit bar, a serve-yourself ice cream bar, and, at breakfast, an omelet bar.

Servery B offers a Deli Line with build-your-own sandwiches, a wokery where diners can choose fresh vegetables and cook them to taste, and a Pan Geos "Cranary" which offers fresh vegetarian flavors from around the world. A Fitness Line offers choices for the nutrition- and calorie-conscious. A homemade pizza bar, pasta bar, cook-to-order omelets, Mexican bar, sundae bar, and burger bar are included.

It's Still the Same Old Story
Romance on the Campus

In the drawing that opens the Senior Class section of the school's first year-book, The Sou'wester of 1899, a graduate of SPU gazes longingly down the woodland path as Dan Cupid takes aim from a nearby tree.

Love by the Numbers

A survey of the all-male student body in 1908 revealed the following romantic preferences:

"Sixty percent admit being in love, although some said they could not help it. Fifty percent prefer brunettes; thirty percent, blondes; and the rest will take both, or anything they can get.
One man said he preferred brunettes, but was in love with both."

LOVE'S COBWEBS

Why do I love you?
   Oh, how can I tell!
I seem to be under
   A strange, magic spell.

Like a fly in a cobweb,
   So I am to-day,
All wound in your weavings,
   And can't get away.

Nor would I untangle
   Myself if I could,
For to be in your web
   Makes a fellow feel good.

BLUE-BOTTLE.

—The 1909 *Sou'wester*

Love in the '40s

Bus Ride in the '50s

Love in the '90s

Love in the '80s

Love in the '90s

Rites of Passage

From the 1920s through the 1950s, freshmen were subjected to a light-hearted initiation process that was called hazing—though it was far from the dangerous and demeaning activities that we think of when we hear the term today.

As Dean A.T. Johnson said in 1953, "It seems to me that hazing, as it exists at Southwestern, is done in the friendliest of spirit and in the interest of facilitating early acquaintanceship between freshmen and upperclassmen."

The theory was that obeying a set of ridiculous rules would bring freshmen together, and that subjecting them to the whims of upperclass students would foster friendships between the classes.

Over the forty years of the observation of these rituals, new students were subjected to several weeks of such "tortures" as wearing funny hats, parading in their pajamas, singing the Alma Mater on request, wearing name placards, not being allowed to walk on the grass on campus, and counting the stones on the terrace of Palmer Hall.

BEDLAM BREAKS FORTH WHEN FROSH PARADE IN PAJAMAS

High Priest Sid Davis Calls Roll of Somber Lads. Raid Hotels, Stop Traffic, Make Heap Noise.

Silence of Court Square was unbroken save for the occasional chirp of a squirrel or the maternal hoot of a pidgeon. Suddenly a blast from a trumpet pervaded the tranquil atmosphere. Then ten robed figures arrived upon the scene. They were soon followed by hundreds of trembling creatures, garbed in the costume of the bedroom.

High Priest Sid Davis, of the San Hedrin, was administering the roll call to the frigidaire victims, after which ceremony they were ushered, amidst the clashing of sabers, into the thoroughfare. The official band of the San Hedrin Council was functioning to perfection. The well known ditty, "The Rambler," was gushing forth from the satanic flutes of the "wind-jammers."

The procession moved on. What was formerly an orderly line of trembling Freshmen was converted into a gesticulating mob of "hoodlums." All of the hotels of importance were visited, clerks held their ears, bell-hops hopped, chamber-maids fainted. They were unaware whether the invaders were a Florida hurricane or an anniversary celebration from Bolivar.

Squire Avent tantalized the knights of the traffic into subjection, while the howling hundreds did their war-dance around the stations of the law guardians, namely, Main and Madison, Union and Main, and Beale Avenue. After many more vocal storms of enthusiasm had been dispensed with, the mob disbanded and the Freshmen adjourned to

The Sou'wester, *October 8, 1926*

Hay! Hay! Farmer Gray's On The Campus

Farmers wear straw hats. Therefore the local freshman had to play in the hay pile on the campus. They were so playful that they operated the baling machine, tossed hay, carried bales, dove into the piles, and in other ways made themselves rural. Some of them enjoyed themselves extremely.

The Sou'wester, *September 23, 1927*

Pajama-clad freshmen tossed their shoes in a pile, then had to race to retrieve them, put them on, and complete the race.

In the '20s, freshmen wore straw hats with their class year on them until the school had won two football games. The hats were then burned in a bonfire. This one escaped.

Despite her proper baby bonnet and name placard, a 1950s freshman is admonished by upperclass women.

Rules for freshmen were spelled out in the 1948-49 Student Handbook.

STAND UP AND CHEER!

Stand up and cheer!
Stand up and cheer for old Southwestern.
For today we raise
The Red and Black above the rest, above the rest.
Our boys are fighting,
And they are out to win the fray.
We've got the steam, rah! rah!
We've got the team, rah! rah!
For this is old Southwestern's day.

FRESHMAN
REGULATIONS AND RULES
for all new
SOUTHWESTERN STUDENTS

All freshman students of Southwestern at Memphis, and all new students of less than junior class standing, are required by the Student Council, through the authority vested in it by the administration of the college, to observe certain regulations which are designed to instill in new students the spirit of the college. Regulations will apply equally to men and women with certain variations.

Familiarization with freshman regulations is the duty of every student who is required to comply with them. The following regulations will take effect on Monday, Sept. 20, at 8:30 in the morning.

1. Standard freshman caps (for boys) and baby bonnets (for girls) must be worn on the campus and in the

buildings, day and night. with the exception that they will not be worn during chapel services, in classrooms, in laboratories, in the student's own home or dorm rooms, or when engaged in athletics.

2. Large, legible signs, at least 8 inches by 12 inches in size, must be worn, bearing the student's name and home town. These signs will be worn at all times on the campus by freshman and transfer alike.

—48—

3. The west and north doors of Palmer Hall may not be used by freshmen or transfers during the hazing period.

4. All freshmen and transfers will sit in the designated seats and wear the designated clothes at all athletic events.

5. No emblems, marks, letters, or pins of high schools may be worn at Southwestern at Memphis.

6. Too much talk from freshmen is definitely undesirable.

7. At no time will freshmen or transfers be allowed to walk on the grass anywhere on the campus, during the hazing period.

8. Freshmen will attempt at all times to grow up.

9. New students will be required to yell certain 'advertisements' between classes as deemed necessary by upperclassmen.

10. Freshmen will speak to everyone on the campus and attempt to learn the names of all the seniors.

11. All new students are required to be able to sing the Alma Mater song by Wednesday morning, Sept. 22.

12. Upon request, a short entertainment after the regular chapel program will be presented by the new students.

13. Freshmen will be held responsible for any questions pertaining to this handbook.

14. Shorts and slacks are not to be worn by women students on the campus, except when participating in athletics or decorating.

15. Freshman women should at all times conduct themselves in a ladylike manner.

16. Freshman and transfer women, when living in or visiting in the dorms, are required to obey all dormitory regulations.

17. By Wednesday, Sept. 22, each new male student will turn in to the Vice-President of the Student Body

—49—

Oh How We Danced . . .

The Tobacco Exchange Building where the SPU fraternities held their Commencement Balls was just five years old in 1885—and the pride of Clarksville.

Heading for the ball, from The Sou'wester *of 1908.*

Balls and Banquets at the Tobacco Exchange

"The Commencement season this year has been enlivened by two highly enjoyable social events. The ATO and the KS fraternities have engaged in a generous rivalry in their annual balls and banquets and each has striven to surpass the other in the brilliancy and sumptuousness of these entertainments.

"The ATO affair came off in the Tobacco Exchange Friday night and was in every particular a complete success. The Maltese Cross included in the decorations was 'a thing of beauty.' The banquet was elaborate. Music was furnished by Wehrley's Legion Band of Louisville.

"The Kappa Sigmas were determined to surpass the Alpha Tau Omegas in their ball of Wednesday night. The Exchange building was again brilliant. The Hall was decorated beautifully with the Crescent and Star emblazoned in gas jets at the entrance of the building. The supper table was set in the figure of St. Andrew's Cross and the banquet was sumptuous. The hours after supper were devoted to the German led by Edgar Morton of New Orleans. The favors were very pretty hand-painted 'sachets.' The Italian Band of Nashville made music for the occasion."
—The Chronicle, June 1885

"The band has got to make noise whether they make music or not."

—A Freshman's English I *Essay on Dancing*, from the *SPU Journal*, March 1914

"At nine-thirty the band has struck up the strains of 'Snookey Ookums' or 'Here Comes My Daddy Now' or some other raggy rag, it takes the peppery stuff to get by now. Anything like 'The Last Days of Pompey' won't do. The band has got to make noise whether they make music or not. They are kept as busy as a bird dog with fleas.

"A modern dance is not like the one our fathers indulged in. They do not have the slightest resemblance to each other. It would be mortifying to the Virginia Reel

This flapper danced though the pages of a Zeta Tau Alpha scrapbook in 1929.

or the Polka to be put into the same class as the Bunny Hug or Turkey Trot. The old and the new style dancing are as far different as the North and South Pole.

"At present the Tango is the rage. This name is derived from the Latin verb 'tango' meaning 'to touch', and believe me, they do touch. This dance includes a collection of dances such as the 'Fish Walk,' 'Jelly Bean,' 'Dip to Heaven,' 'Kangaroo Slip,' 'Castle Walk,' and many others.

"Many of the present dances come by their names by their resemblances to certain animals. We notice in this case the 'Grizzly Bear,' 'Lame Duck,' 'Turkey Trot,' and 'Bunny Hug.' Several dances got their names from the places that had the honor to produce them. As the 'Texas Tommie,' 'South Bend,' 'Boston Dip,' 'Mobile Mop Up,' etc. To be a good tango dancer you have to be limber and able to stick through the whole fray. Otherwise you have no more chance then an English Sparrow has of wrecking a battleship. Thus is a modern dance put on."

Jitterbuggers took the floor in 1940.

A retro dance in the '70s celebrated the bop style of the '50s.

The Panhellenic Dance, 1962

In January 1998, the 150th Anniversary Ball brought the entire college community together in a celebratory mix of ages, dance styles, and dance wear.

The Sigma Nu Spring Formal of 1937 offered a plaque as a memento to the guests.

Chapter Eleven: Student Life

"A student's responsibility
to his college does not end on
Commencement day . . ."
—Dr. Marion Edmund Melvin, Class of 1900

Beyond Fisher Garden, high above the crowd of commencement well-wishers, a departing message for graduating seniors rings from Halliburton Tower. As the striker hits the side of the tower's bronze bell, the T.S. Eliot quote inscribed on the bell's inside wall finds voice in the gong of metal upon metal. "Not fare well," the inscription cautions, "but fare forward, voyagers."

Graduation is not the end of a partnership but the beginning of the most durable of relationships: the alliance between Rhodes and her alumni. As Dr. Marlon Edmund Melvin, member of the Class of 1900 and President of Missouri's Westminster College, noted in his address to alumni during the Jubilee and Inaugural Celebration in November 1925:

"A student's responsibility to his college does not end on Commencement day, but lasts as long as he lives . . . . A College lives in its Alumni."

Students' transition to alumni status begins in Fisher Garden, the site of commencement ceremonies since 1942.

March 1929

October 1974

Spring 1994

Alumni: The Collective Body

"Thy torch has touched our hearts with flame."

—Rhodes Alma Mater

The Rhodes Time Line

This Time Line of the College's history was developed by Martha Shepard for her 150th Anniversary issue of Rhodes magazine. The design was created by Trey Clark and Kevin Barré.

Castle Building

Forbes

Stewart

Robb Hall

Clarksville, Tennessee 1848-1925

1848 Clarksville Academy becomes Masonic University of Tennessee

1849 W.F. Hopkins, president, college doors open for first time.

1850 Castle Building completed, William A. Forbes, president

1851 Charter secured for Montgomery Masonic College

1853 William M. Stewart, president

1855 Synod of Nashville purchases Montgomery Masonic College, renames it Stewart College

1858 R.B. McMullen, president

1860 Robb Hall, first dormitory, completed

Wilson

1896 Football Team

Summey

1898-99 Basketball Team

Woods

Dinwiddie

Dobyns

1885 Dr. Joseph R. Wilson, father of Woodrow Wilson, heads new School of Theology

1888 C.C. Hersman, chancellor

1891 J.M. Rawlings, chancellor, first mention of a football team

1892 George Summey, chancellor

1898 New gym opens, men's basketball first played

1899 First Homecoming football game vs. Sewanee

1904 Federal Government awards College $25,000 for damages during Civil War

1905 Neander M. Woods, chancellor, board allows women to attend classes, but not earn credit

1908 William M. Dinwiddie, chancellor

1914 Chancellor now called President; J.R. Dobyns, president

1931 Hall of Fame

Commencement in Fisher Garden

Cadets

The Shacks

Rhodes

1951-Lynx Lair Opens

Burrow Library

1928 Honors courses established; Future U.S. President Herbert Hoover awarded honorary doctor of laws

1931 Hall of Fame established in Palmer, heresy charges against Dr. Diehl, tutorial system begins

1936 Football team defeats Vanderbilt 12-0; Singers organized

1942 First Commencement in new Fisher Garden

1943 Army Air Force cadets train on campus; Adult Education Center (later Meeman Center) organized; First woman editor of Lynx—Anne Howard Bailey

1945 First woman student body president—Mary Ann Banning; "Man" course introduced; College renamed Southwestern At Memphis

1947 "Temporary" buildings— the shacks— constructed (photo circa 1969)

1948 Voorhies Hall dedicated; First Algernon Sydney Sullivan Award presented

1949 Peyton N. Rhodes, president, Phi Beta Kappa installed

1953 Burrow Library dedicated

Dressed for dinner

Bowden

Soccer

Daughdrill

Anthony Sculpture

Palmer Roof

McCoy Theatre

1968 Frazier Jelke Science Center, Glassell Hall dedicated, coat and tie dinner rule abolished

1969 Women's dorm curfew ends

1970 William L. Bowden, president; Clough Hall dedicated; Southwestern at Oxford (later British Studies) initiated

1971 Hyde Gymnasium dedicated; Men's soccer team organized

1973 James H. Daughdrill Jr., president

1975 Golden Anniversary of opening in Memphis

1977 Dedication of Alburty Swimming Complex; Lawrence Anthony campus sculpture completed

1980 Williford Hall dedicated; first Rites of Spring; Palmer Hall roof needs first repair since 1925

1981 Clarence Day Awards for Teaching and Research established; McCoy Theatre dedicated

1983 Diehl Court dedicated

1861
All but two students enter Confederate Army

1862
Civil War closes college, occupied by Union Troops

1865
College colors adopted—cardinal and black

Shearer

1869
Stewart College reopens

1870
J.B. Shearer, president

SPU Seal

1874
Synods of Presbyterian Church assume control of college

1875
College renamed Southwestern Presbyterian University

Stewart Hall

1877
Stewart Hall begun

1878
First Greek fraternity established, Pi Kappa Alpha

Waddell

1879
President now called chancellor, John N. Waddel, chancellor

Diehl

1916
Board votes to admit women on same terms as men

1917
Charles E. Diehl, president

1918
Sou'wester first published as a weekly

1920
Synods approve college move to Memphis

Patch

1921
Margaret Trahern Patch, first woman graduate

1922
First sorority established—Chi Omega

1924
Lynx becomes mascot

Cloister under construction

Memphis 1925–

1925
College moves to Memphis, Yearbook renamed Lynx

Rollow Avenue of Oaks

1927
Omicron Delta Kappa established, seedlings from Clarksville campus planted—today's Rollow Avenue of Oaks

---

Mallory Gym

1954
Mallory Gymnasium dedicated

Orgill Bowl

1955
Orgill Bowl first presented in Sewanee/Southwestern football rivalry; Townsend Hall dedicated; International Studies Program begins with grant from Carnegie Corp.

1956
Ellett Hall dedicated; Danforth Program established (became the Kinney Program) President's Residence at 671 West Dr. purchased

President's Home

1958
Catherine Burrow Refectory dedicated

1961
Bellingrath and Townsend Halls dedicated

Townsend Hall

1962
Moore Moore Infirmary and Halliburton Tower dedicated

Halliburton Tower

1963
Board votes to admit all students on an equal basis

1964
Mortar Board installed

Alexander

1965
John David Alexander, president

mastodon

1966
Dilemma established; Thomas W. Briggs Student Center dedicated; mastodon remains unearthed at Frazier Jelke excavation

---

1984
Board votes to change name to Rhodes College, Hassell Hall dedicated

Benefactors' Circle

1985
Benefactors' Circle dedicated in Cloister

1986
"Man" course now called "Search;" King Hall, the old Pi Kappa Alpha national headquarters, purchased

Lynx sculpture unveiled

1987
Campus Green organized; Spann Place dedicated; Ann Moore Nunnery '88 completes Lynx sculpture

1990
Iron fence completed around perimeter of campus

Buckman Hall

1991
Buckman Hall dedicated

1992
President's House at 91 Morningside Park purchased

91 Morningside Park

1996
Dedication of Blount Hall

1997
Dedication of Bryan Campus Life Center

Bryan Campus Life Center

1998
College celebrates Sesquicentennial Year